Katrina

Devastation. Survival. Restoration.

A Unique Look Through the Eyes of 40 Photojournalists

The Times

*TUESDAY, AUGUST 30, 2005
SHREVEPORT • BOSSIER CITY • ARK-LA-TEX

shreveporttimes.com

Catastrophic
Gulf Coast awash in misery of Hurricane Katrina

Bryan Vernon and Dorthy Bell of New Orleans are rescued from their rooftop after Hurricane Katrina hit, causing flooding in their neighborhood Monday. Officials called for a mandatory evacuation of New Orleans, but many residents remained in the city.

shreveporttimes.com
Go online for the latest on Hurricane Katrina
► View photo galleries
► Learn how you can help
► Get local shelter updates
► Read regional newspapers

Tell us your story
Send The Times your Hurricane Katrina stories by e-mailing ttumer@gannett.com or by calling (318) 459-3293.

Shelters near capacity

Military aids in relief

Cooking up a storm

Hurricane Katrina
EXTRA
The Clarion-Ledger
Real Mississippi
clarionledger.com

Tuesday, August 30, 2005   Jackson, Miss. ■ 50¢

DECIMATED
80 dead, damage to coast in billions

Sam Miller, 10, left, is consoled by a neighbor after viewing the destruction of his home along Beach Boulevard in Pascagoula, Monday, after Hurricane Katrina passed over the Gulf Coast.
William Colgin, AP Photo/The Press-Register

Flooding, wreckage, death sweep Miss.

Little communication

THE TOWN TALK
www.thetowntalk.com

Tuesday, August 30, 2005   Alexandria-Pineville, Louisiana   ★ 50 Cents

HURRICANE KATRINA

| BLANCO TO EVACUEES: STAY PUT. A6 | OLLA OPENS ARMS TO EVACUEES. A3 | EVACUEES GIVE BOOST TO CENLA ECONOMY. B6 |

Katrina leaves
A BIG MESS

Killer Katrina floods N.O., pounds Miss.
By Allen G. Breed
Associated Press

BY THE NUMBERS

4 Category level of Hurricane Katrina when it made landfall early Monday.

28 In feet, feared storm surge of Katrina around New Orleans.

15 In feet, actual storm surge, which was still enough to cause Lake Pontchartrain to flood one-story houses up to the rooftine.

22 In feet, recorded storm surge in Bay St. Louis, Miss., which was among the hardest-hit areas.

11 Deaths blamed on Katrina when it made its initial landfall in southern Florida Thursday.

59 Deaths so far blamed on Katrina Sunday and Monday: three nursing home residents interred in Baton Rouge, a Concordia Parish resident, 03 in Mississippi and two in Alabama.

870,000 Entergy and Cleco customers without electricity.

70 Price, in dollars, of crude oil futures traded early Monday on an all-time high.

AREADEATHS
Huey P. Seligard Cecilia
Annie R. Bloom
Luke Charles
Alice E. Brown

1 dead, another injured as Katrina approached
By Mandy N. Goodnight
mgoodnight@thetowntalk.com
(318) 487-6465

DAILY World
OPELOUSAS, LA.   TUESDAY, AUGUST 30, 2005   50 CENTS ★

Hurricane Katrina

'God's got our back'
Parish residents assist those fleeing storm; New Orleans hit hard, spared Armageddon scenario; Mississippi Gulf Coast devastated

Photo by Freddie Herpin
The halls of learning at Opelousas Senior High School were turned into halls of refuge Monday as the school housed several hundred evacuees fleeing the fury of Hurricane Katrina.

INSIDE
■ See Page 4A
Refugees flock to St. Landry Parish.
■ Little damage reported locally.

■ See Page 5A
Southeast Louisiana residents find safe haven in St. Landry Parish.

■ See Page 6A
■ N.O. still standing.
■ Superdome's roof punctured; refugees take shelter.
■ French Quarter beaten, battered ... but unbowed.

■ See Page 7A
■ Storm deals 'grievous blow' to Mississippi.
■ Towering surf pounds Alabama beaches.

Index
Classified ... 5B
Crossword ... 2B
Opinion ... 4A
Horoscope ... 2B
Movies ... 3B
Obituaries ... 7A
Sports ... 1B

How to reach us

Area pours heart out to hurricane refugees
By Aldo A. de la Villesbret and Lana Ardoin

Katrina spikes gas, oil prices
Bush may dip into reserves
By The Associated Press

Continuous coverage @ www.theadvertiser.com
News updates • Aerial photos and galleries • Send us your stories

THE DAILY ADVERTISER
www.theadvertiser.com

Wednesday, August 31, 2005   50 cents ★

■ **Out of control:** Looting spreads in downtown New Orleans. Page 2A
■ **Scenes:** Images of the catastrophic wake of Katrina. Pages 6B, 7B
■ **Disbelief:** Evacuees see the first photos of the destruction at home. Page 4A
■ **Settling in:** Evacuated students can register in Lafayette. Page 4A

PANIC RISES

In New Orleans, despair sets in
By Kayla Gagnet
kgagnet@theadvertiser.com

'Dome becomes home to refugees'
By Kayla Gagnet
kgagnet@theadvertiser.com

Rising water adds to survivors' woes
By Claire Taylor

The Times
SHREVEPORT • BOSSIER CITY • ARK-LA-TEX

*WEDNESDAY, AUGUST 31, 2005
shreveporttimes.com

Despair, horror
Level of devastation still rising

Floodwaters fill the streets of New Orleans on Tuesday. More photos, 8A, 9A.

shreveporttimes.com
► Expanded coverage
► Local shelters
► How to help
► Photo galleries

Tell us your story
Send The Times your Katrina stories by e-mailing ttumer@gannett.com or by calling (318) 459-3293.

Water among worries

Police send help south

Evelyn Turner cries alongside the body of her husband, Xavier Bowie, after he died in New Orleans on Tuesday. Bowie and Turner had decided to ride out Hurricane Katrina when they could not find a way to leave the city.

'My city is gone'
By Don Walker
dcowalker@gannett.com

Helping hands reach

Contents

This book represents the collective efforts of 40 photojournalists from the Gannett Newspapers in Mississippi and Louisiana, and nine other Gannett newsrooms. The foreword was written by The Clarion-Ledger Executive Editor, Ronnie Agnew and Assistant Managing Editor, Debbie Skipper. Chapter introductions were written by Billy Watkins and Orley Hood, both from The Clarion-Ledger.

Gavin Averill *Hattiesburg American* Hattiesburg, Miss.	**Craig Bailey** *Florida Today* Melbourne, Fla.	**Shane Bevel** *The Times* Shreveport, La.	**Bart Boatwright** *Greenville News* Greenville, S.C.	**Joel Bonner** *Hattiesburg American* Hattiesburg, Miss.	**Janet Braswell** *Hattiesburg American* Hattiesburg, Miss.	**Brian Albert Broom** *The Clarion-Ledger* Jackson, Miss.	**Denice Broussard** *The Daily Advertiser* Lafayette, La.	**Matthew Bush** *Hattiesburg American* Hattiesburg, Miss.	**Arely D. Castillo** *The News-Star* Monroe, La.

Bill Clark *Gannett News Service* Washington, D.C.	**George Clark** *Hattiesburg American* Hattiesburg, Miss.	**Helen Comer** *The Jackson Sun* Jackson, Tenn.	**Margaret Croft** *The News-Star* Monroe, La.	**Karen S. Doerr** *Montgomery Advertiser* Montgomery, Ala.	**Michael Dunlap** *The News-Star* Monroe, La.	**John F. Elbers II** *Rockford Register Star* Rockford, Ill.	**Joe Ellis** *The Clarion-Ledger* Jackson, Miss.	**Barbara Gauntt** *The Clarion-Ledger* Jackson, Miss.	**Tony Giberson** *Pensacola News Journal* Pensacola, Fla.

Paris L. Gray *Courier-Post* Cherry Hill, N.J.	**Rick Guy** *The Clarion-Ledger* Jackson, Miss.	**Jim Hudelson** *The Times* Shreveport, La.	**Greg Jenson** *The Clarion-Ledger* Jackson, Miss.	**Brad Kemp** *The Daily Advertiser* Lafayette, La.	**Katie King** *Pensacola News Journal* Pensacola, Fla.	**Vickie King** *The Clarion-Ledger* Jackson, Miss.	**Claudia B. Laws** *The Daily Advertiser* Lafayette, La.	**Jessica Leigh** *The Times* Shreveport, La.	**Ian Morrison** *The News-Star* Monroe, La.

Greg Pearson *The Times* Shreveport, La.	**Patrick Peterson** *Florida Today* Melbourne, Fla.	**Peter C. Piazza** *The Daily Advertiser* Lafayette, La.	**John Rowland** *The Daily Advertiser* Lafayette, La.	**Robert Ruiz** *The Times* Shreveport, La.	**J.D. Schwalm** *The Clarion-Ledger* Jackson, Miss.	**Mike Silva** *The Times* Shreveport, La.	**Natasha Smith** *Hattiesburg American* Hattiesburg, Miss.	**Randy Snyder** *The Herald-Dispatch* Huntington, W.Va.	**Chris Todd** *The Clarion-Ledger* Jackson, Miss.

Copyright© 2006 • ISBN: 1-59725-053-8 (Louisiana)   ISBN: 1-59725-052-X (Mississippi)

Foreword

Hurricane Katrina was the storm we always feared in Mississippi and Louisiana.

We've endured others, but we never thought we'd live to witness such power, such destruction, such force stretching hundreds of miles into different states into different lives, sparing few along its devastating journey.

In one day, Katrina obliterated homes, hospitals, schools, businesses and communities in Louisiana and on the Mississippi Gulf Coast. In two states that had seen glimmers of hope in their decades-long battle against poverty, the Aug. 29 storm created a whole new underclass: working-class people left homeless, hungry and in the unfamiliar role of asking for help.

In Mississippi, a 70-mile stretch of coastline laid waste, 236 dead, an estimated $125 billion in damage, and 65,380 houses destroyed.

Mississippi Coast residents ran like people in Third World countries after trucks throwing bottles of water, diapers, bread and other supplies. They wandered dirty and stunned through the wreckage of once thriving communities. They saw the homes on which they are still paying mortgages reduced to slabs of concrete, and the insurance policies for which they'd faithfully paid their premiums for years deemed worthless. They didn't yell or beat their breasts or unleash an endless stream of blame. They pitched tents, they sifted through the debris, they tried to live again.

To the west, a different story emerged in Katrina. The proud city of New Orleans, a place of jazz, dancing and happy times, fell into a sad state.

Some blamed a lack of planning. Some blamed residents who didn't take the storm seriously. Some blamed leadership for the lack of an evacuation plan. Whatever the problems, the result was deadly. Some 1,500 people died because of Katrina; the unaccounted for still number into the thousands.

New Orleans' standing as one of this country's flagship cities took a pounding after the storm, as much for the city's response to the disaster as the disaster itself. The famous Superdome became more than a shelter, it became a microcosm of urban problems seething beneath the surface.

An entire nation wept after viewing scenes of elderly residents, already weakened and battered by time, walking along deserted roadways in search of help. For some, help never came and their final resting place was on cold hard streets.

But Katrina's strength didn't stop there. To say that would be to diminish just how destructive the killer storm actually was.

Everyone was affected by this hurricane. People residing in towns such as Hattiesburg, Miss., and Laurel, Miss., people residing in one Louisiana parish after another. All have stories to tell about Katrina.

Governors wept openly because of Katrina, unable to express to their residents the full scope of the devastation.

There was once a Waveland, Miss., until Katrina came along. The tiny town, perhaps the hardest hit along the Mississippi Gulf Coast, lost everything – its landmarks, its streets and too many of its residents.

The dead are among the people who had ridden out storms before, brave souls who thought the strength of plywood would hold off yet another one, brave souls who had the indignity of resting in refrigerated tractor trailers while search and rescue efforts went on.

But the Katrina story is as much a story about resilience as it is about disaster. People are picking up the remnants of their broken lives, piece by piece. Towns are rebuilding again. There is enough commerce to keep economies in Mississippi and Louisiana humming for years to come. Sadness and hope. Destruction and construction. Death and life.

They are the things this monster storm has left us. We won't be caught off guard again. Katrina has taught us that deadly lesson. Never again.

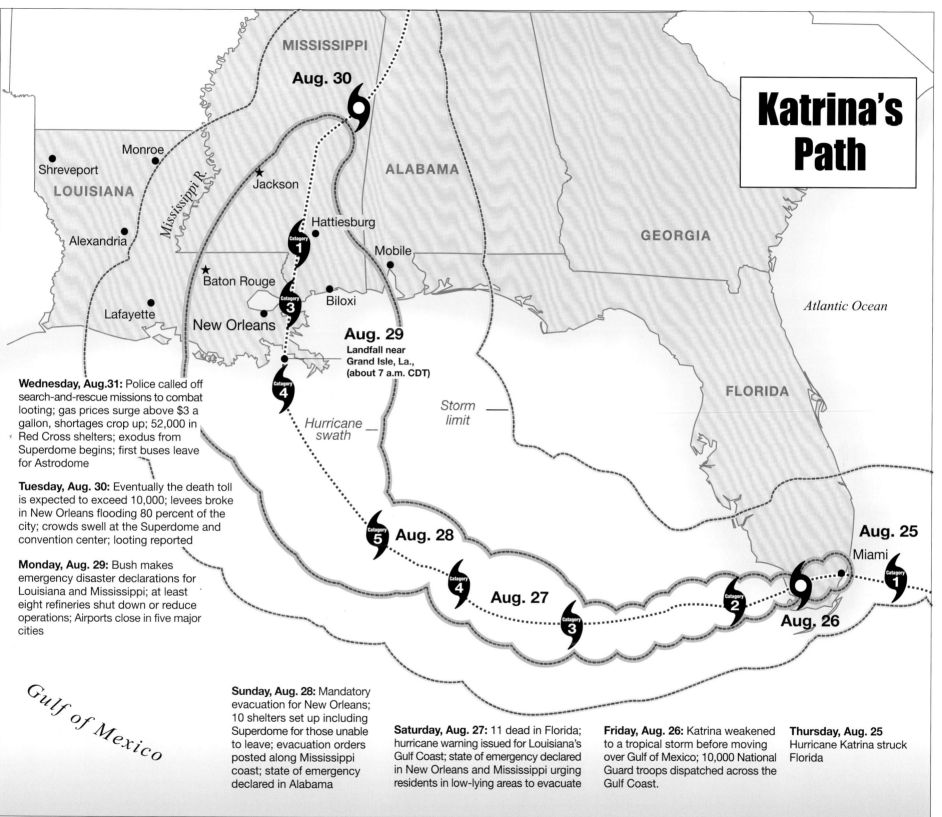

Katrina's Path

MISSISSIPPI

Aug. 30

ALABAMA

LOUISIANA

Shreveport

Monroe

Mississippi R.

★ Jackson

Hattiesburg

Catagory 1

Mobile

Alexandria

★ Baton Rouge

Catagory 3

Biloxi

Lafayette

New Orleans

GEORGIA

Atlantic Ocean

Aug. 29
Landfall near
Grand Isle, La.,
(about 7 a.m. CDT)

Catagory 4

FLORIDA

Storm limit

Hurricane swath

Wednesday, Aug.31: Police called off search-and-rescue missions to combat looting; gas prices surge above $3 a gallon, shortages crop up; 52,000 in Red Cross shelters; exodus from Superdome begins; first buses leave for Astrodome

Tuesday, Aug. 30: Eventually the death toll is expected to exceed 10,000; levees broke in New Orleans flooding 80 percent of the city; crowds swell at the Superdome and convention center; looting reported

Monday, Aug. 29: Bush makes emergency disaster declarations for Louisiana and Mississippi; at least eight refineries shut down or reduce operations; Airports close in five major cities

Catagory 5 **Aug. 28**

Aug. 25

Miami

Catagory 4 **Aug. 27**

Catagory 2

Catagory 1

Catagory 3

Aug. 26

Gulf of Mexico

Sunday, Aug. 28: Mandatory evacuation for New Orleans; 10 shelters set up including Superdome for those unable to leave; evacuation orders posted along Mississippi coast; state of emergency declared in Alabama

Saturday, Aug. 27: 11 dead in Florida; hurricane warning issued for Louisiana's Gulf Coast; state of emergency declared in New Orleans and Mississippi urging residents in low-lying areas to evacuate

Friday, Aug. 26: Katrina weakened to a tropical storm before moving over Gulf of Mexico; 10,000 National Guard troops dispatched across the Gulf Coast.

Thursday, Aug. 25 Hurricane Katrina struck Florida

SOURCES: AP research; FEMA; Red Cross; GNS

Dennis Lowe, FLORIDA TODAY / GNS Gulf Coast map

The Storm

As he stood on a Biloxi beach around noon on Aug. 27, 2005, Jim Cantore felt the Gulf of Mexico gently lapping at his ankles, like a playful puppy.

He promised things were about to change, that a major hurricane named Katrina was dead-aimed at the Mississippi Gulf Coast. "I hope it weakens," said The Weather Channel's most recognizable meteorologist, "and I hope I'm wrong."

He wasn't. Two days later, the Category 3 storm, with sustained winds of 127 miles per hour and packing a storm surge nearly four times larger than most hurricanes its size, killed 231 in Mississippi and destroyed thousands of homes and businesses in the coastal towns of Waveland, Bay St. Louis, Pass Christian, Long Beach, Gulfport, Biloxi, Ocean Springs, Gautier and Pascagoula.

Residents and city officials in New Orleans expressed relief as the storm's dangerous east side skirted past them. But the next day, up to 18 inches of rain in some areas caused a break in the levee system, which was supposed to protect New Orleans from Lake Pontchartrain and the Mississippi River. The Big Easy, known for fine cuisine and world-class jazz, was covered in nasty, stinking water. Approximately 1,100 died and thousands lost their homes. Helicopters plucked dozens of helpless residents from their roofs and attics.

In December, approximately 1,300 others still were "feared dead"; that would make Katrina the second-deadliest natural disaster in United States history. More than 8,000 died in the hurricane that hit Galveston, Texas, in 1900.

Property damage caused by the storm is estimated at more than $200 billion.

Katrina was massive, a Category 5 (winds exceeding 155 mph) during one point in its journey through the Gulf. Katrina's surge — the unyielding wall of water deposited onto the Mississippi Coast — was estimated at more than 30 feet high, causing many to drown along the coastline. Katrina showed little mercy as it barreled northward. Hattiesburg endured 120 mph winds; Jackson 75.

Thousands in Louisiana, Mississippi and Alabama were left without electricity. Food, water and gasoline became precious commodities.

New Orleans, located between 5 and 10 feet below sea level, saw the flood it had feared for decades come to life.

And a new benchmark for hurricanes invading Mississippi had been established. Camille, a 1969 Category 5 that killed 172 with its 250 mph winds and storm surge of 25 to 27 feet, had been outdone.

Many didn't believe that was possible.

Many of those died.

■ **LEFT:** Palm trees sway as winds from Hurricane Katrina hit Cypremort Point, La. *Claudia B. Laws/The Daily Advertiser*

■ **RIGHT:** Dardenella Clark rushes through the rain to find a stall for her pet Chihuahua, "Sassy'" at the Forrest County Multi Purpose Center as Hurricane Katrina reaches Hattiesburg, Miss., on Monday, Aug. 29. People using the shelter as a refuge from Hurricane Katrina were allowed to use the horse pens at the Multi Purpose Center to house their pets for the duration of the storm. *Gavin Averill/Hattiesburg American*

■ **FAR LEFT:** Donnie Braud, manager of Southern Fassiner in Houma, La., boards up the store on Sunday morning, Aug. 28, as Houma residents prepare for the worst. *John Rowland/The Daily Advertiser*

■ **LEFT:** A convenience store in Houma, La., is packed with people buying any food available as Katrina bears down on the community Sunday afternoon. *John Rowland/The Daily Advertiser*

■ **ABOVE:** Millard Leedy is filling gas cans as he makes preparations to stay in Houma, La., on Sunday morning. *John Rowland/The Daily Advertiser*

■ **RIGHT:** Volunteer firefighters Wendy Gautreaux and Captain Conrad Harlan, in Houma, La., add to a sign that says "Katrina have mercy on us." New Orleans Mayor Ray Nagin issued a mandatory evacuation order for New Orleans. The firefighters added "everyone get out." *John Rowland/The Daily Advertiser*

■ **BELOW:** Curley Calloway sits on his porch in Houma, La., on Sunday morning as he plans to ride out the storm at home. *John Rowland/The Daily Advertiser*

■ ABOVE: The storm is being tracked in the office of emergency preparedness in Houma, La., on Sunday, Aug. 28, as Katrina approaches. *John Rowland/The Daily Advertiser*

■ LEFT: Sid Johnson, co-owner of Beautiful Day CD Exchange, boards up his store in preparation for Hurricane Katrina in Hattiesburg, Miss., on Sunday, Aug. 28. *Gavin Averill/Hattiesburg American*

■ BELOW: Karen Pinner (center, in red) of Lacombe, La., joins a group of family and friends in prayer inside the lobby of the Holiday Inn Express Hotel on Greymont Avenue in Jackson, Miss., where scores of Gulf Coast evacuees gathered to get TV news updates (background) as Hurricane Katrina made landfall on Monday morning. Lopreore said that their group of about 15-20 people were able to get a block of four rooms at the hotel where they will remain until authorities give the all-clear to return to Louisiana. *Joe Ellis/The Clarion-Ledger*

■ **ABOVE:** The northbound lanes of Highway 90 from New Orleans are packed with cars as they try to escape from the path of Katrina on Aug. 28. *John Rowland/The Daily Advertiser*

■ **RIGHT:** Contra-flow traffic heads northbound in all lanes on I-59 as evacuees from New Orleans flee Hurricane Katrina on Aug. 28. *George Clark/Hattiesburg American*

■ **FAR RIGHT:** Sebastian Martinez, 6, of New Orleans looks over a map of the state while his family rents a large car at the Alamo Rent-A-Car to evacuate New Orleans. *Claudia B. Laws/The Daily Advertiser*

■ **ABOVE:** Five year old Trevon Mitchell is pulling his luggage into the Houma Terrebonne Civic Center in Louisiana as his family looks for a spot to settle in on Sunday afternoon, Aug. 28. *John Rowland/The Daily Advertiser*

■ **LEFT:** Bayou Black residents Gene Bergeron (left) and Lacey Bonbillian sit in the Houma Terrebonne Civic Center in Louisiana on Sunday afternoon as they take shelter from Katrina. *John Rowland/The Daily Advertiser*

■ ABOVE: Olivia Beasley of Houma gives her son Jyron Beasley a kiss as they rest in the Houma Terrebonne Civic Center in Louisiana on Sunday afternoon. *John Rowland/The Daily Advertiser*

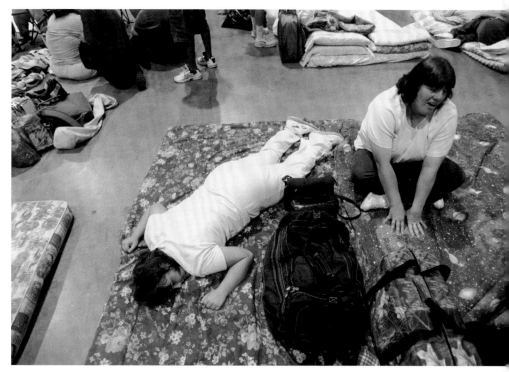

■ ABOVE & LEFT: Hundreds found shelter at the Mississippi Coliseum in Jackson as Hurricane Katrina reached Category 5 status Monday morning, Aug. 29. *Vickie King/The Clarion-Ledger*

■ RIGHT: Fifteen year old Ashley Stinson tries to make herself comfortable with her mother Veronica Stinson (right) on the concrete floor of the Houma Terrebonne Civic Center in Louisiana on Sunday afternoon, Aug. 28. *John Rowland/The Daily Advertiser*

■ RIGHT: Dale Ledet, left, and Robert Lawrimore, right, lean into the wind while staying at the Red Cross shelter in the Forrest County Multi Purpose Center after the eye of Hurricane Katrina passed Hattiesburg, Miss., on Monday, Aug. 29. *Gavin Averill/Hattiesburg American*

■ FAR RIGHT: Angela Bly of Madison, Miss., braves high wind and rain to get gas at the Shell station in Madison. "I'm afraid the pumps are going to go down...the electricity." *Barbara Gauntt/The Clarion-Ledger*

RIGHT: Dante Brown of Jackson, Miss., stands outside his house "just testing how high the wind is" as his mother Barbara Brown Williams stands laughing inside the door.
Barbara Gauntt/The Clarion-Ledger

FAR RIGHT: Front desk associate Mike Keeley moves furniture away from a blown-out window on the fifth floor of the Hawthorne Suites Hotel in Hattiesburg, Miss., as Hurricane Katrina approaches the area on Monday, Aug. 29. Windows blew out of two rooms before noon with the eye of the storm still more than an hour away.
Bill Clark/Gannett News Service

BELOW: An emergency vehicle makes its way around a downed tree on N. Main Street in downtown Hattiesburg, Miss., early Monday, Aug. 29. *Bart Boatwright/Greenville News*

The Aftermath

The day after, at dawn's early light, it was time to take inventory. What was left?

Officials reached back to the last weeks of World War II, to Japan and the atomic bombs, to find suitable comparisons.

"Right now downtown (Gulfport) is like Nagasaki," Harrison County FEMA director Col. Joe Spraggins said.

"I can only imagine what Hiroshima looked like 60 years ago," Mississippi Gov. Haley Barbour said.

In New Orleans, so fragile and vulnerable, all was well — for a moment. Then levees broke. Lake Ponchartrain gushed over and through, filling the city with a toxic goop. The Superdome crowded with the stranded and the desperate. Police communications were lost. Chaos broke out. In the end, 300,000 homes would be destroyed or rendered uninhabitable in New Orleans and St. Bernard Parish.

A half million Mississippians awoke to a world without electricity, without phone service of any kind, without potable water. Without ...

Waveland. Where was Waveland?

In the first week of September it became more apparent that Katrina had caused devastation on a biblical scale. From Ocean Springs west, through Biloxi and Gulfport, into Bay St. Louis and Long Beach, to the Louisiana line and beyond, from the beach two miles inland to the railroad tracks, virtually nothing had been spared.

■ **LEFT:** Raphael Siguencia (left) and Demetrio Cuevas, both of Biloxi, Miss., survey the damage to the Ocean Springs-Biloxi Bridge. Both men are employees of the destroyed Grand Casino in Biloxi. Siguencia is thinking about returning to Ecuador and Cuevas is thinking of returning to Mexico as there is no work on the Mississippi Gulf Coast for the two. *Brian Albert Broom/The Clarion-Ledger*

■ **RIGHT:** Sylvie Campbell fights back tears after seeing her mother-in-law's piano in her New Orleans home. The Campbells came back to the home for the first time to retrieve jewelry and whatever photos they could salvage. *Shane Bevel/The Times*

Homes, lives and history were lost. In a few nightmarish hours, evidence of three centuries of coastal life disappeared. Wedding pictures, high school annuals, diaries, histories — gone.

Rescue and recovery crews counted the dead — 1,070 in New Orleans, 231 in Mississippi, found over several weeks and months — and tended to the living.

Two weeks later, the Rev. Michael Tracey would tell his parishioners at Our Lady of the Gulf Catholic Church in Bay St. Louis, "You are alive because your work is not finished. We are here for a reason. We will rebuild."

Not just buildings, but dreams.

■ **ABOVE:** A neighborhood along Howard Avenue in Biloxi, Miss., received total destruction. The height of the surge forced boats into the trees. The aftermath of Hurricane Katrina will last for years. Entire neighborhoods were turned into match sticks and the grim search for bodies continues. *J.D. Schwalm/The Clarion-Ledger*

■ **RIGHT:** The remains of shipping containers from the port of Gulfport litter the beachfront of Gulfport, Miss., after Hurricane Katrina blew through the previous week. The return to normal is slowly taking place as streets are cleared and power is restored. *J.D. Schwalm/The Clarion-Ledger*

■ **ABOVE:** Debris piled high where a home once stood at 224 Farrar Lane in Waveland, Miss. Home after home was destroyed during Hurricane Katrina for about a full mile inland. *Jim Hudelson/The Times*

■ **LEFT:** High winds and storm surge moved a section of the Grand Casino (foreground) in Gulfport, Miss., to the center of U.S. 90. *Joe Ellis/The Clarion-Ledger*

■ **BELOW:** The Copa Casino barge ended up on a parking lot after Katrina hit the Mississippi Gulf Coast. *Joe Ellis/The Clarion-Ledger*

■ **LEFT:** In Hattiesburg, Miss., motorists create a long line on U.S. 49 at I-59 to buy gas. *J.D. Schwalm/The Clarion-Ledger*

■ **FAR LEFT:** A low land neighborhood on the Mississippi Gulf Coast remains flooded two days after Katrina hit. *Joe Ellis/The Clarion-Ledger*

■ **ABOVE:** Cars under water on West End Boulevard from flooding by Hurricane Katrina, Tuesday, Aug. 30, in Metairie, La.
Brad Kemp/The Daily Advertiser

■ **RIGHT:** A street sign in Metairie, La., sits in high water left behind by the flooding. *Greg Pearson/The Times*

■ **BELOW:** Two people float down a street in a canoe in Metairie, La., to survey the damage. *Greg Pearson/The Times*

■ **ABOVE:** A destroyed apartment building along Hwy. 90 in Biloxi, Miss., is framed by a tattered American flag at a business next to the apartments. *Jim Hudelson/The Times*

■ **LEFT:** A field of debris is all that is left of what used to be apartment buildings on the barren slabs of concrete from this neighborhood on the Mississippi Gulf Coast. *Joe Ellis/The Clarion-Ledger*

■ **ABOVE:** A set of bench seats is all that remains of a Waffle House restaurant in Gulfport. Gulf Coast homes and business were completely obliterated. *Randy Snyder/The Herald-Dispatch*

■ **RIGHT:** Paul Slayton clears debris from the entrance to The Mirage clothing store on Canal Street in New Orleans. The store lost 95 percent of its merchandise to flooding and looting. *Shane Bevel/The Times*

■ **FAR RIGHT:** An interstate is a temporary staging area as thousands of evacuees wait in the rain at Interstate 10 and the Causeway outside of New Orleans to be moved to shelters. *Jessica Leigh/The Times*

■ **ABOVE:** The front steps are all that remain of a building destroyed by Hurricane Katrina in front of the University of Southern Mississippi Gulf Park Campus in Long Beach, Miss.   *Gavin Averill/Hattiesburg American*

■ **RIGHT:** A building is exposed after its windows were blown out by the powerful winds of Hurricane Katrina.   *Greg Pearson/The Times*

■ **FAR RIGHT:** After destroying houses within a few blocks of U.S. 90 and the beach, Katrina's storm surge pushed the debris inland almost covering some houses on the Mississippi Gulf Coast.

Joe Ellis/The Clarion-Ledger

■ **BELOW:** The Hurricane Camille monument in Biloxi, Miss., was also damaged during Hurricane Katrina. Biloxi, Miss., residents had church service earlier in the day behind the monument.

Karen S. Doerr/Montgomery Advertiser

LEFT: Looters fill Canal Street on Tuesday Aug. 30. With no police presence many stores on the street are being ransacked.
John Rowland/The Daily Advertiser

FAR LEFT: The intersection of 10th and Pontchartrain Blvd. is covered with flood water from Hurricane Katrina, Tuesday, Aug. 30, in New Orleans. *Brad Kemp/The Daily Advertiser*

■ **ABOVE:** Looters load grocery carts with goods and hustle out of Rouse's Supermarket in Metairie, La. Looting of food and drinks ran wild in Metairie and Jefferson Parish. Deputies arrested some people after seeing that appliances and non-necessities were being stolen.
Jessica Leigh/The Times

■ **RIGHT:** Forrest Paper Co. in Hattiesburg, Miss., was heavily damaged by Hurricane Katrina.
George Clark/Hattiesburg American

■ **FAR RIGHT:** General Manager Ray Rejkowski surveys damage to the Tire Center after Hurricane Katrina's passage through Hattiesburg.
Joel Bonner/Hattiesburg American

■ **FAR LEFT:** Piles of cars and debris washed into downtown Biloxi, Miss., during Hurricane Katrina. *Brian Albert Broom/The Clarion-Ledger*

■ **LEFT:** The Lake Pontchartrain light house, left, and the Southern Yacht Club in New Orleans, Sept. 2, after they were destroyed by Hurricane Katrina. *Brad Kemp/The Daily Advertiser*

■ **BELOW:** Pictured from left to right, Melissa Halliday, Bobby Ryals, Tiffany and Rebecca Cole all of Hattiesburg, Miss., talk with the University of Louisiana at Monroe level four nurse Wendy Vansaagsvelt. *Michael Dunlap/The News-Star*

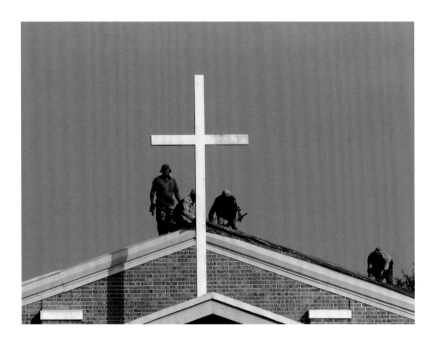

■ **ABOVE:** Workers secure temporary tarps on the roof at the First Pentecostal Church along Hwy. 21 in Bogalusa, La. *Jim Hudelson/The Times*

■ **RIGHT:** Bob Rue, owner of Sarouk Shop on Erato and St. Charles in New Orleans posted a sign outside his store warning looters that they will suffer consequences if they attempt to rob his store. Looting has begun to spin out of control in and around New Orleans. *Jessica Leigh/The Times*

■ **BELOW:** Debris has been pushed clear of the roads in Waveland, Miss., just a few blocks from the Gulf of Mexico. *Jim Hudelson/The Times*

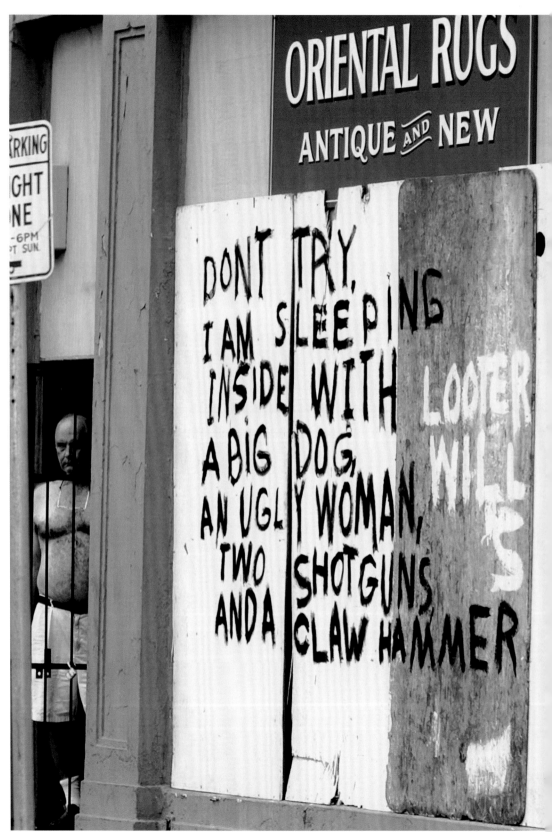

■ **ABOVE:** Destroyed neighborhood in Chalmette in St. Bernard Parish, La.
Robert Ruiz/The Times

■ **LEFT:** Standing in the wreckage of what was their living room, Sam (right) and Mae Woo sift through the debris in search of family mementos weeks after Katrina passed through eastern Belzoni, Miss., leaving a swath of destruction in its wake. Mae Woo said that the couple had lived in the house for 27 years.
Joe Ellis/The Clarion-Ledger

■ **BELOW:** Jaques Freret uses a crowbar to open a door to the flooded home of his girlfriend in New Orleans, Saturday, Oct. 2. *Brad Kemp/The Daily Advertiser*

■ **ABOVE:** Abandoned rescue boats line Archbishop and St. Bernard Highway in Meraux, La., as flood waters begin to recede. *Claudia B. Laws/The Daily Advertiser*

■ **RIGHT:** Baptist Memorial Hospital patients with pets are bused out of New Orleans, at Napoleon and St. Charles to be moved to shelters. *Jessica Leigh/The Times*

ABOVE & LEFT: Flood waters and wind damage from Hurricane Katrina devastate a subdivision off Florida Avenue in Chalmette, La.

Claudia B. Laws/The Daily Advertiser

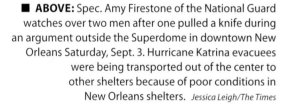

■ **ABOVE:** Spec. Amy Firestone of the National Guard watches over two men after one pulled a knife during an argument outside the Superdome in downtown New Orleans Saturday, Sept. 3. Hurricane Katrina evacuees were being transported out of the center to other shelters because of poor conditions in New Orleans shelters. *Jessica Leigh/The Times*

■ **RIGHT:** Capt. Jesse Stewart and other soldiers with the 82nd Airborne guard the gates at Charity Hospital in New Orleans. The hospital is being cleaned and drained, but bodies still remain in the flooded basement morgue. *Shane Bevel/The Times*

■ **FAR RIGHT:** Thomas Shannon, 43, of Marrero, La., lays on top of a pile of garbage outside the Superdome in downtown New Orleans Saturday, Sept. 3, as the Hurricane Katrina evacuees are being transported out of the center to other shelters because of poor conditions in New Orleans shelters. *Jessica Leigh/The Times*

■ **ABOVE:** Trees uprooted by the hurricane in Hattiesburg, Miss., on Wednesday Aug. 31.
Tony Giberson/Pensacola News Journal

■ **ABOVE RIGHT:** Traffic creeps around the debris left scattered by Hurricane Katrina as motorists drive south on I-59 north of Hattiesburg, Miss.
George Clark/Hattiesburg American

■ **RIGHT:** The home of Gene Reimert was destroyed by Hurricane Katrina and still has trees on it on Tuesday, Sept. 6, eight days after the Hurricane damaged Hattiesburg, Miss. *Gavin Averill/ Hattiesburg American*

■ **ABOVE:** Men pick through rubble as a boat sits several hundred yards from the beach in Biloxi, Miss., historic downtown district. Storm surge from Hurricane Katrina destroyed many of the old buildings in the area. *Rick Guy/The Clarion-Ledger*

■ **LEFT:** One camp stands in the rubble of the dozens that were destroyed on Grand Isle, La. *Peter C. Piazza/The Daily Advertiser*

■ **FAR LEFT:** William Murdock sits amid what's left of his home at 1612 E. Beach Boulevard, in Gulfport, Miss., looking for salvageable items. Most of the homes along the historic street were destroyed or heavily damaged when Hurricane Katrina tore through the area. *Rick Guy/The Clarion-Ledger*

■ **ABOVE:** Smoke from uncontrolled fires rises over New Orleans as water from broken levees starts to flood the streets. *Peter C. Piazza/The Daily Advertiser*

■ **RIGHT:** A view of New Orleans the day after Hurricane Katrina hit. Smoke from fires fills the sky as the streets were just beginning to flood. *Peter C. Piazza/The Daily Advertiser*

■ **FAR RIGHT:** New Orleans and New York firefighters battle a fire as a helicopter drops foam on the blaze at a home on Royal Street in New Orleans on Tuesday, Sept. 6. *Jessica Leigh/The Times*

■ **RIGHT:** A woman sits on an air mattress at the newest Red Cross shelter inside Hirsch Memorial Coliseum on the Louisiana State Fairgrounds in Shreveport, La. *Greg Pearson/The Times*

■ **BELOW:** The Louisiana Superdome is surrounded by flood waters in New Orleans. *Greg Pearson/The Times*

■ **ABOVE:** Numerous buildings in Hattiesburg, Miss., show the effects of Hurricane Katrina on Monday, Aug. 31. *Tony Giberson/Pensacola News Journal*

■ **ABOVE LEFT:** Darmesha Miller stands guard near groceries outside of Rouse's Supermarket in Metairie, La., that her family took from the store. Looting of food and drinks ran wild in Metairie and Jefferson Parish. Deputies arrested some people after seeing that appliances and non-necessities were being stolen. *Jessica Leigh/The Times*

■ **LEFT:** Surrounded by spoiled and smashed food, Hannah El Saadawy and her son, Fahtima, sit outside of Rouse's Supermarket in Metairie, La., as they wait for Hannah's husband to return from inside the store with groceries.
Jessica Leigh/The Times

■ **ABOVE:** The lower floor of this home on East Beach Boulevard in Gulfport, Miss., was completely destroyed by Hurricane Katrina.
Gavin Averill/Hattiesburg American

■ **LEFT:** Residents of the Hattiesburg, Miss., Howard Johnson's Motel look at the damage left by the collapse of a brick wall caused by Hurricane Katrina as it passed through the area on Monday, Aug. 29. *Bill Clark/Gannett News Service*

■ **FAR LEFT:** Ed Throop walks away from the rubble of his home on East Beach Boulevard in Gulfport, Miss., on Saturday, Sept. 2. *Gavin Averill/Hattiesburg American*

■ **ABOVE:** Flooded cars in the parking lot of the PHI heliport in Port Sulphur, La., after Hurricane Katrina. *Peter C. Piazza/The Daily Advertiser*

■ **LEFT:** Aerial of a flooded used car lot in Covington, La., as the water begins to go down. *Peter C. Piazza/The Daily Advertiser*

■ **FAR LEFT:** A damaged gas well burns in the Gulf of Mexico off of Plaquemines Parish, La.
Peter C. Piazza/The Daily Advertiser

■ **ABOVE:** Debris filled the streets of Arabi, La., which was flooded after a levee failed.
Peter C. Piazza/The Daily Advertiser

■ **RIGHT:** A levee break drains the floodwater out of upper Plaquemines Parish.
Peter C. Piazza/The Daily Advertiser

■ **BELOW:** This is the first street from the Mississippi River in the Lower Ninth Ward, New Orleans. Directly behind these houses is where the levee broke. *Robert Ruiz/The Times*

■ **ABOVE:** Tug boats and barges sit on the Mississippi River levee south of New Orleans after Hurricane Katrina. *Peter C. Piazza/The Daily Advertiser*

■ **LEFT:** Fishing boats sit on the ramp of the Hwy. 23 bridge in Plaquemines Parish, La. *Peter C. Piazza/The Daily Advertiser*

■ **ABOVE:** Three weeks after the landfall of Hurricane Katrina, a marina on the shores of Lake Pontchartrain still lays in waste with sailboats scattered among the slips. *Shane Bevel/The Times*

■ **RIGHT:** Flooded school buses in Plaquemines Parish, south of New Orleans. *Peter C. Piazza/The Daily Advertiser*

■ **FAR RIGHT:** Abandoned boats still sit piled up in the Violet Canal in St. Bernard Parish, La. Parish officials have been watching Hurricane Rita and preparing for another hit. *Shane Bevel/The Times*

■ **ABOVE:** Leeland Martin pulls his brother Milton Martin to the Superdome on an inflatable mattress on Tuesday afternoon, Aug. 30. *John Rowland/The Daily Advertiser*

■ **RIGHT:** Water starts to flood the area around the Superdome the morning after Hurricane Katrina passed due to broken levees. *Peter C. Piazza/The Daily Advertiser*

■ **BELOW:** Myrtis Clark is with her dogs as she paddles her way across New Orleans to check on her mother. *John Rowland/The Daily Advertiser*

■ **LEFT:** Reese Pursell is prepared to defend his Canal Street business with a bat as bands of looters roam the streets.
John Rowland/The Daily Advertiser

■ **BELOW:** "We'll be back," promises a sign on the historic Mary Mahoney's restaurant in downtown Biloxi, Miss. The former Brunet-Fourchy House built in 1895 suffered major damage. *Patrick Peterson/Florida Today*

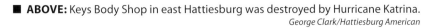

■ **ABOVE:** Keys Body Shop in east Hattiesburg was destroyed by Hurricane Katrina.
George Clark/Hattiesburg American

■ **ABOVE:** A fallen Pine tree has literally cut this house in half. Most of the damage in Mandeville, La., resulted from falling trees, not flooding.
John Rowland/The Daily Advertiser

■ **RIGHT:** Trees uprooted by Hurricane Katrina lay scattered on the front lawn of the University of Southern Mississippi in Hattiesburg, Miss., on Monday, Aug. 29. *Gavin Averill/Hattiesburg American*

■ **FAR RIGHT:** Orville Ferrell of Waveland, Miss., took time to visit some friends making shelter in what remains of downtown Waveland, Miss. The small town of 7,000 was practically destroyed. Relief efforts were beginning to ease the misery on the Mississippi Gulf Coast. The Waveland/Bay St. Louis area in Mississippi received extreme damage. *J.D. Schwalm/The Clarion-Ledger*

■ **ABOVE:** Contractor Wayne Hughes of Winnsboro, Tex., reads one of the Hurricane Katrina stories left on the trunk of a huge water oak felled by the storm in Hattiesburg, Miss. Bob and Betty Press hope to preserve the stories as a community resource. *Janet Braswell/Hattiesburg American*

■ **LEFT:** Fishing boats jammed on the side of the Hwy. 23 bridge in Plaquemines Parish, La. *Peter C. Piazza/The Daily Advertiser*

■ **FAR LEFT:** Yacht harbor destruction from Hurricane Katrina as seen on Oct. 2 in New Orleans. *Brad Kemp/The Daily Advertiser*

■ **BELOW:** Concrete steps lead up to a demolished trailer at Mary Ann Trailer Park in Meraux, La. *Claudia B. Laws/The Daily Advertiser*

■ **ABOVE:** The Pelican Bay Condominiums in Biloxi, Miss., had the first two floors completely gutted by Hurricane Katrina. *Rick Guy/The Clarion-Ledger*

■ **RIGHT:** A group of firemen check out a demolished home off Beach Boulevard in Gulfport, Miss. Most of the homes along the historic street were destroyed or heavily damaged when Hurricane Katrina tore through the area. *Rick Guy/The Clarion-Ledger*

■ **ABOVE:** Asst. Chief Marvin Howard (right) receives a briefing on the search by California Task Force #4 lead by Rich Dickinson during operations in Biloxi, Miss. The search continues for bodies in the Point Cadet area where massive destruction took place.
J.D. Schwalm/The Clarion-Ledger

■ **LEFT:** Hurricane Katrina damage on Brookmead Boulevard at Timberlane Estates in the Terrytown area in Louisiana.
Claudia B. Laws/The Daily Advertiser

■ **FAR LEFT:** Paula Perri pauses from a fruitless search for some of her belongings in the rubble of her apartment destroyed by Hurricane Katrina in Gulfport, Miss., on Saturday Sept. 2, five days after the hurricane damaged the city.
Gavin Averill/Hattiesburg American

■ **ABOVE:** Andy Mayfield, 74, of Hattiesburg, Miss., views the remains of his kitchen, which was crushed when a giant tree came through it during Katrina, taking out the entire side of his house. He and his wife, Carolyn, cannot get to their food or refrigerator because of debris.

Katie King/Pensacola News Journal

■ **RIGHT:** Danny Smith of Biloxi, Miss., searches the area near his home at Point Cadet in an attempt to locate fishing nets and any other personal items he could find. The apartment building that was near his home was washed away. He clung to a nearby tree for several hours as flood waters swirled around the fallen limbs. He did find a reel for a fishing pole. He calls the stairs the "stairway to heaven."

J.D. Schwalm/The Clarion-Ledger

■ **ABOVE:** Betty Robinson searches the remains of her sister's business in an effort to salvage anything left after it was destroyed by Hurricane Katrina. Relief efforts were beginning to ease the misery on the Mississippi Gulf Coast. *J.D. Schwalm/The Clarion-Ledger*

■ **ABOVE:** Hurricane Katrina damage on Colony Road at Timberlane Estates in the Terrytown, La., area. *Claudia B. Laws/The Daily Advertiser*

■ **RIGHT:** Hurricane Katrina damage at a Burger King in Gretna, La. *Claudia B. Laws/The Daily Advertiser*

■ **FAR RIGHT:** John Macfarland of Waveland, Miss., holds a photo of what his house once looked like while standing in his driveway. He evacuated to Pensacola, Fla., with his wife only to return to total destruction. He knows the situation is bad in New Orleans, but he feels the total loss of homes in the Gulf Coast area have not been receiving much needed attention. *J.D. Schwalm/The Clarion-Ledger*

■ **ABOVE:** Debris left behind by evacuees is piled along Interstate 10 at the Causeway Boulevard exit on Sept. 3.
John Rowland/The Daily Advertiser

■ **LEFT:** A brick building collapsed on Camp Street in New Orleans.
John Rowland/The Daily Advertiser

■ **FAR LEFT:** The Superdome is now a ghost town inhabited only by police, military and an occasional stray dog.
Greg Pearson/The Times

ABOVE: David Sackler, owner of Sack's Outdoors, makes plans on what to do next as his sons try to secure his business that suffered severe damage from looters. Sackler, who had boarded up all of his windows, said that Hurricane Katrina did more damage to his store than any other hurricane in his 54 years of business. *George Clark/Hattiesburg American*

RIGHT: Hurricane Katrina flattened the Episcopal Church of the Redeemer in Biloxi, Miss. The church's bronze bell that survived Hurricane Camille, rests on the ground beside plaques bearing the names of those killed by Camille. *Patrick Peterson/Florida Today*

FAR RIGHT: John Sanders of Biloxi, Miss., sits on the debris-filled Front Beach in Biloxi. Sanders says he and his wife lost everything including her job to Hurricane Katrina and they don't know what to do. *Brian Albert Broom/The Clarion-Ledger*

The People

Some chose to stay and ride out Katrina; others had no choice, either because they owned no vehicle or couldn't afford $2-a-gallon gas to put in it.

In the end — whether people along the Louisiana-Mississippi Gulf Coast stayed or evacuated, owned a little before the storm or a lot — nearly everyone had part of their everyday lives ripped away.

Normalcy vanished. There was an urgent plea for baby formula — stores were closed, stock was ruined, babies were going hungry.

New Orleans, where floodwaters swallowed houses and parts of the downtown district, turned into the Wild West. Water-logged bodies were placed in black bags and stacked like firewood at two collection sites, awaiting identification. Lawbreakers and police officers exchanged gunfire. Armored military vehicles were called in to restore order.

More than 20,000 took refuge at the city's convention center and inside the Louisiana Superdome, where sweat once fell from players during six Super Bowls but now poured from people trying to survive relentless 90-degree heat. They were left there for days — hot, hungry, thirsty, some say forgotten. Fires, fights and

shootings were reported. Finally, they were evacuated by bus, mainly to the Astrodome in Houston, Texas. A cot and three meals a day awaited them.

But the storm also brought out the good in people. Churches and schools across the Southeast set up shelters for evacuees. Families opened their homes to strangers in need.

"This whole thing showed us we're not in control of anything," said David Boyd, 26, of Long Beach, Miss. "No matter how good we think we've got it, we're always at the mercy of God — and of each other."

■ **LEFT:** Kimberly Copus, of Buras, La., cries after speaking to her sister on the phone for the first time since she fled Hurricane Katrina. Copus, her two sons and her father, with whom she was recently reunited, fled Buras on Sunday and arrived at the Red Cross Shelter at the Forrest County Multi Purpose Center in Hattiesburg, Miss., on Friday, Sept 2.
Gavin Averill/Hattiesburg American

■ **RIGHT:** Jamie and Susan Thompson of Petal, Miss., reflect on the last few days during Sunday services at Petal Harvey Baptist Church.
Craig Bailey/Florida Today

■ **RIGHT:** Tammy Louis and her husband Henry Louis (seated), thank Orlando Chapman for their dinner. Chapman, owner of Brother's Seafood in Shreveport, La., provided free food for evacuees from Hurricane Katrina at his restaurant. The Louis family is from Madisonville, La.
Jim Hudelson/The Times

■ **BELOW:** Devin Chuckwuonu, of Beaumont, Miss., waits in line for the second time for gas at a Shell station on U.S. 98 West in Hattiesburg, Miss. The line for gas was approximately an hour-and-a-half long. Volunteers also helped man the pumps. *Helen Comer/The Jackson Sun*

■ **ABOVE:** Gisele (G.G.) Brown (right), is reunited with friend Bernie Barnett in Hattiesburg, Miss. Brown, was staying in the Red Cross shelter at the Forrest County Multi Purpose Center. *Matthew Bush/Hattiesburg American*

■ **ABOVE:** Kim Jimmerson holds Z'Kayla Raymond who has been sick since she got to Lafayette, La., on Thursday, Sept. 1. Jimmerson traveled here with 22 other people in a dairy truck from New Orleans. *Denice Broussard/The Daily Advertiser*

■ **ABOVE LEFT:** Geannie McDonald of New Orleans watches footage of her hometown in the aftermath of Hurricane Katrina on a television in the LSU gymnasium. *Greg Pearson/The Times*

■ **LEFT:** Arion Landry says, "I miss my daughter." She is staying at the shelter at Hooter Park in Bossier City, La., and lived in New Orleans. Her daughter is with her mother in Alabama. *Mike Silva/The Times*

LEFT: Rob Scriver of Gulfport, Miss., says retrieving an old cart from nearby woods and making a sign was all he knew to do. Scriver said his mobile home was severely damaged by Hurricane Katrina and with no transportation, he cannot get to area food and supply distribution points. Many others face the same problem on the Mississippi Gulf Coast due to a lack of fuel.
Brian Albert Broom/The Clarion-Ledger

FAR LEFT: Living in a donated tent and depending on donations and relief aid, the strain shows on the face of Patricia Pawlak of 128B Oak Street in Biloxi, Miss., who barely survived Hurrricane Katrina and lost everything she owned. *Brian Albert Broom/The Clarion-Ledger*

BELOW: "I can't do this again," says Lacombe, La., evacuee Jane Lopreopre (right) to her husband Mario (left) while standing in the line for Red Cross assistance at the Mississippi Trademart in Mississippi for the second day in a row. The Hurricane Katrina assistance isn't for them. It is for Mario Lopreopre's parents, who lost everything in their St. Bernard, La. home. Lopreopre's father had received a pacemaker a month ago and is now in Texas undergoing surgery for the malignant cancer they found during the pacemaker operation. *Barbara Gauntt/The Clarion-Ledger*

■ **ABOVE:** Congressman Bobby Jindal of Louisiana talks with Robert Berthelot of St. Bernard parish outside the Office of Emergency Preparedness in Baton Rouge, La. Berthelot lost his hotel in Hurricane Katrina and wanted to get some help as well as offer it as a staging area or temporary shelter. *Greg Pearson/The Times*

■ **RIGHT:** Despite no longer being able to work at the Grand Casino in Biloxi, Miss., Uriel Alvarado says he likes the area and plans to stay as he cooks chicken over a fire in front of his destroyed apartment building on US 90. *Brian Albert Broom/The Clarion-Ledger*

■ **BELOW:** Diane Quin and her fiance Buddy Curry, from the New Orleans area, organize their truck in the parking lot at the LaQuinta in Bossier City, La. The couple arrived the previous morning with reservations and had a room for the night. *Jim Hudelson/The Times*

■ **ABOVE:** Joseph Baxter's favorite tree, a giant Loblolly pine that measured 13 feet in circumference and was 105 feet tall, was toppled during Hurricane Katrina. Baxter, who lost more than 100 trees on his property in the Epley community near Sumrall, Miss., would like to see the wood from this tree put to good use. *George Clark/Hattiesburg American*

■ **LEFT:** President George W. Bush (center) walks with Homeland Security Secretary Michael Chertoff (left) and Lt. Gen. Russel Honore as they make their way into the Office of Emergency Preparedness in Baton Rouge, La. *Greg Pearson/The Times*

■ **ABOVE:** Hurricane Katrina evacuee Gale Bradford weeps about her mother, Irene Barabin, after they were separated at the Superdome in downtown New Orleans Saturday, Sept. 3. Evacuees were transported from the center to other shelters with better living conditions.

Jessica Leigh/The Times

■ **RIGHT:** Angela Willis irons her clothes while getting ready to go to work at Horseshoe Casino in Bossier City, La. Willis worked at the Harrah's casino in New Orleans but is currently staying in the Employee Welcome Center at Harrah's Louisiana Downs in Bossier City with other employees from Harrah's casinos affected by Hurricane Katrina.

Jim Hudelson/The Times

■ **FAR RIGHT:** "I was trying to get home to Hammond after visiting my brother in Durham, North Carolina and ran into this. Amtrak got to Birmingham and gave us a choice: we could go back or go on forward on the bus. Since I was already heading forward, I took Greyhound to here; been here since about midnight Saturday," said Sam Carter, as he caught up on the latest storm news while camped out at the Mississippi Coliseum in Jackson, Miss. *Vickie King/The Clarion-Ledger*

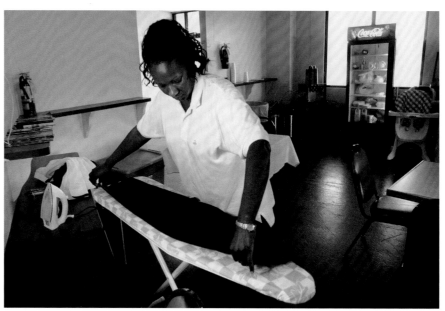

■ **ABOVE:** Jake Hecht, 16, gives away apples to drivers waiting for supplies at the Bass Academy in Purvis, Miss. *Paris L. Gray/Courier-Post*

■ **RIGHT:** Angela King, 28, of Hattiesburg, Miss., with the Air National Guard, says she is worried more about the state of others around the community than she is of the loss of her bedroom, which was destroyed when a giant tree came crashing through the ceiling during Hurricane Katrina. "Everything is fixable," she said. *Katie King/Pensacola News Journal*

■ **BELOW:** Rose Williams (center in pattern top with brown pants) prays with family and friends who are staying in her and other relatives homes in Haughton, La., because of Hurricane Katrina. *Jim Hudelson/The Times*

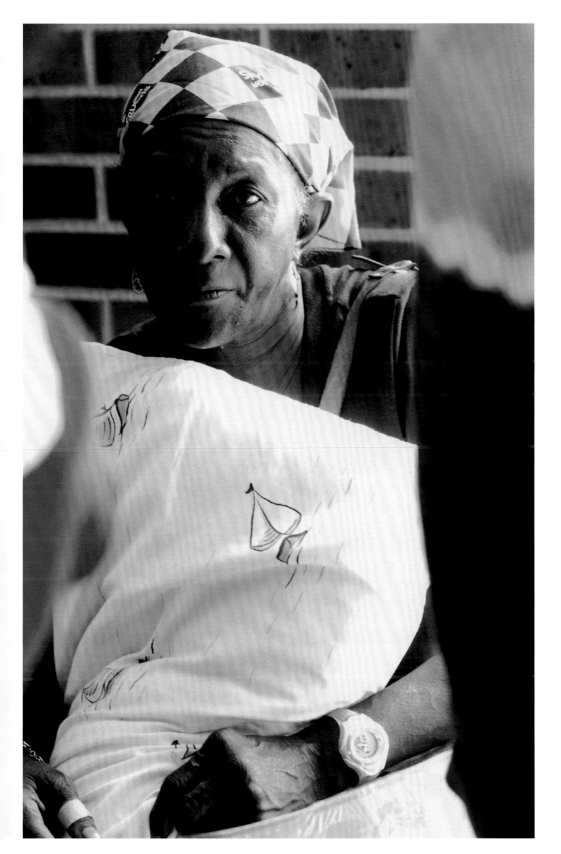

■ **ABOVE:** Matilda Magee of Magnolia, Miss., rests her eyes while sitting outside the Mississippi Trademart in Jackson while waiting on friends who are standing in a nearby line to get assistance from the Red Cross. Magee and her mother arrived at the Trademart well before dawn and made their way through the line just before 10 a.m. but had to wait on their friends who had given them a ride from Magnolia.

Joe Ellis/The Clarion-Ledger

■ **LEFT:** New Orleans evacuee Aslee Washington spends time sitting outside of the Cajundome in Lafayette, La. Washington is still trying to find out what happened to three of her children, Sandra, Ashawanna and Ronald Washington.

Claudia B. Laws/The Daily Advertiser

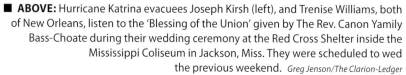

■ **ABOVE:** Hurricane Katrina evacuees Joseph Kirsh (left), and Trenise Williams, both of New Orleans, listen to the 'Blessing of the Union' given by The Rev. Canon Yamily Bass-Choate during their wedding ceremony at the Red Cross Shelter inside the Mississippi Coliseum in Jackson, Miss. They were scheduled to wed the previous weekend. *Greg Jenson/The Clarion-Ledger*

■ **RIGHT:** Sister Jacyntha Nguyen prays for people who are suffering because of Hurricane Katrina on Monday, Aug. 29. Sister Nguyen is a Hurricane Katrina evacuee from New Orleans to Monroe, La. *Arely D. Castillo/The News-Star*

■ **FAR RIGHT:** Melvin Bush, lifelong resident of Algiers, explains how the historic area of New Orleans got its name Monday, Sept. 19. *Michael Dunlap/The News-Star*

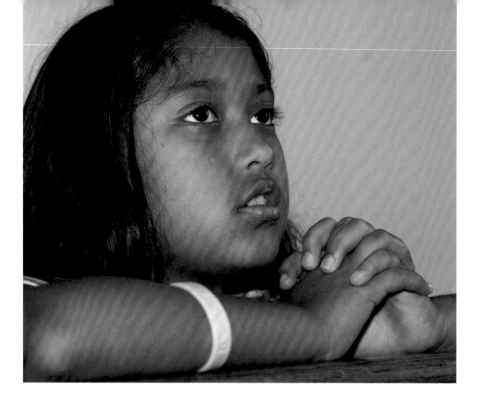

■ **ABOVE:** Katrina evacuee Ivania Vallejo, 9, of Honduras prays during service at St. Alban's Episcopal Church on Sunday, Sept. 18, in Monroe, La. Vallejo and her family lived in Kenner, La. *Arely D. Castillo/The News-Star*

■ **RIGHT:** Tom Arcineaux prays from one of the pews inside First United Methodist Church in Shreveport, La. The church welcomed people to come in and pray in response to Gov. Kathleen Blanco's naming the day as a day of prayer. *Greg Pearson/The Times*

■ **BELOW:** Norma Winegart kneels in front of the altar to pray at First United Methodist Church in Shreveport, La. *Greg Pearson/The Times*

■ **ABOVE:** Gloria Thomas, 70, said she was too old to be bused all around the country and sleep on the floor. She was waiting at Southern University Shreveport for a bus back to the Cajun Dome in Lafayette, La. *Mike Silva/The Times*

■ **LEFT:** Fr. Dennis Hayes of New Orleans sits in an office that has become his temporary home at the Office of Emergency Preparedness headquarters in Chalmette, La. Hayes escaped his home with his rosary in one pocket and a cross in the other; nothing else. He later returned to get his dog, Badooki, and a few possessions. Hayes has been counseling volunteers working in the area. *Claudia B. Laws/The Daily Advertiser*

■ **ABOVE:** Broadmoor Baptist Church Pastor Rob Futral (left), gets a hug and applause from Hurricane Katrina evacuees Elton Warren of New Orleans (center), and Jason Alphonso of Chalmette, La., after their testimonials during services on Highland Colony Parkway in Madison, Miss. "That brother really can hug," Rev. Futral said. About 1,700 people, including evacuees, attended two morning services at Broadmoor. *Greg Jenson/The Clarion-Ledger*

■ **RIGHT:** Cajundome resident Mark Kately of New Orleans laughs as he talks to his daughter at the Cajundome in Lafayette, La. Kately was celebrating his birthday by helping a friend he met at the Cajundome run errands. *Claudia B. Laws/The Daily Advertiser*

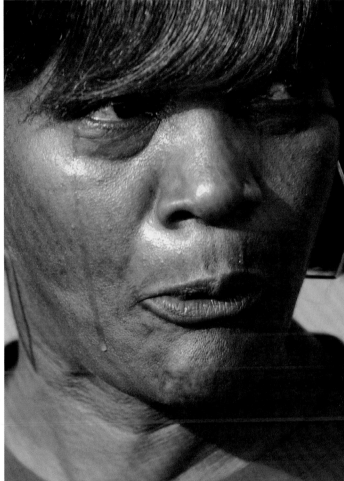

■ **ABOVE:** Linda McGill starts to cry while talking about what she and her family have experienced while waiting in line at the Lamar County Mulit Purpose facility in Purvis, Miss. to get help from the Red Cross on Thursday, Sept. 15. *Paris L. Gray/Courier-Post*

■ **LEFT:** Nathaniel Strange, 2, drinks the last drops from his water bottle while playing outside the Forrest County Multi Purpose Center shelter in Hattiesburg, Miss.
Katie King/Pensacola News Journal

■ **FAR LEFT:** Big Buddy program volunteer Ura Whitner, left, hugs Tyreek Love, 14 months, in Baton Rouge, La., outside a local shelter on Sunday, Sept. 4, as everyone says goodbye to seven children who were separated from their parents during Hurricane Katrina rescues. The volunteers cared for the kids until their parents were notified by the National Center for Missing and Exploited Children and a flight was arranged for them to be reunited in San Antonio, Tex. *Jessica Leigh/The Times*

■ **ABOVE:** Hurricane Katrina evacuees lie in stretchers at Monroe Regional Airport hangar after they were transported by airplane from New Orleans to Monroe, La., on Sunday Sept. 4. *Arely D. Castillo/The News-Star*

■ **RIGHT:** Carol Brown, of New Orleans, holds up a photograph of her son Corey Brown, 13, as she calls Red Cross Hotline searching for information about his whereabouts while staying in the Red Cross shelter at the Forrest County Multi Purpose Center in Hattiesburg, Miss., on Tuesday, Sept. 6. Carol Brown, mother of three children, fled the city to avoid flooding. *Gavin Averill/Hattiesburg American*

■ **BELOW:** Joycelyn Johnson holds her son Michael while her other son Tyerese stands by her outside of the New Iberia shelter in the Cyr-Gates Community Center. Johnson had just tried to contact her relatives with a cell phone from a local phone company and could not get through. Johnson has no idea where the rest of her family is. *John Rowland/The Daily Advertiser*

■ **ABOVE:** Hattiesburg Police Chief David Wynn talks with curfew violation detainees at the Hattiesburg Police Department.
John F. Elbers II/Rockford Register Star

■ **LEFT:** Joyce Andollina breaks down in tears while waiting for a ride with her husband, Clement, and dog, Tootsie, to leave New Orleans and move to shelters. *Jessica Leigh/The Times*

■ **BELOW:** Sharon Blackwell, a dispatcher for Covington County, Miss., handles a call. Blackwell is also a school employee at Covington County schools. *Matthew Bush/Hattiesburg American*

■ **ABOVE:** Louisiana State Police Trooper Doug Pierrelee (right) talks with Herbert Johnson (bottom left) and Vernell Lockett outside the Le'Dale Hotel in New Orleans. Pierrelee asked them about their health, food and water levels, and explained to them the dangers of staying in the city. *Greg Pearson/The Times*

■ **RIGHT:** Johnny Kain of Lacombe, La., looks over his house and backyard after cleaning dead fish from the area Friday, Sept. 2. Kain's garage and yard were damaged the most and he was unsure why so many fish were dying. *Jessica Leigh/The Times*

■ **FAR RIGHT:** Nellie Brooks, who is from New Orleans east, washes her clothes in Priest Creek beside the shelter set up in the Forrest County Multi Purpose Center in Hattiesburg, Miss., Wednesday, Aug. 31. *Bart Boatwright/Greenville News*

■ **ABOVE:** Bartender Larry Hirst, right, serves customers at Johnny White's Sports Bar and Grill on Bourbon Street in New Orleans on Tuesday, Sept. 6. Johnny White's was one of only two bars open for business on Bourbon Street.
Jessica Leigh/The Times

■ **RIGHT:** Lisa Lewis of Tampa, Fla., bathes one of the dogs in the Humane Society shelter at Hattiesburg's Multi Purpose Center. Lewis took a week of vacation to come help.
Craig Bailey/Florida Today

■ **FAR RIGHT:** Katrina evacuees Tess Kearn and Peter Migliccio walk after getting married on Tuesday, Sept. 15, at the Farmerville Recreation Center in Farmerville, La.
Arely D. Castillo/The News-Star

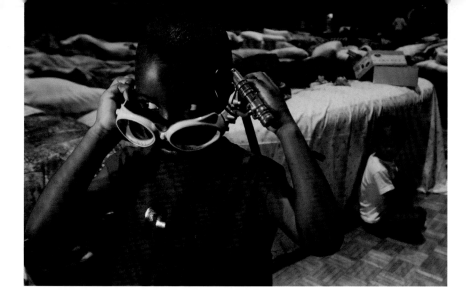

■ **ABOVE:** Allen Coleman III, 3, plays with googles and toys that were donated to the shelter at Hooter Park in Bossier City, La. His family is from New Orleans. *Mike Silva/The Times*

■ **RIGHT:** Shaddai Livingston and Malaika Livingston sit at the kitchen counter while June Phillips prepares dinner in Phillips' North Shreveport, La., home full of family from Hurricane Katrina. *Jim Hudelson/The Times*

■ **BELOW:** Edward Kou, 15, Lovetee Kou, 6, and Vlandy Koudee, 16, all talk with Betty Henderson (in red) and Mary Ann Selber (right) about various supplies and other things that need to be done to get the family situated into their apartment. The family, from Metairie, La., and the two volunteers from the Providence House in Shreveport, La., who are serving as the 'family advocates' for the family who just got into an apartment at Colony Square Apartments. *Jim Hudelson/The Times*

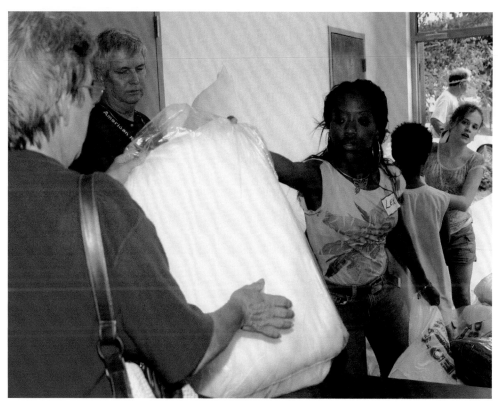

■ **ABOVE:** Alexis Bright, 16, of New Orleans gives towels and pillows to Hurricane Katrina evacuees staying at Monroe's Civic Center on Monday, Aug. 29. Bright is an evacuee as well. *Arely D. Castillo/The News-Star*

■ **ABOVE:** LaShonda Lofton, 23, right, a waitress at Barnhill's Buffet on Hardy Street in Hattiesburg, Miss., and Jessica Touchstone, 32, middle, a volunteer, serve a mass of local people free, homestyle-cooked meals of fried chicken, catfish and hot veggies outside of the restaurant, which was damaged from Katrina.
Katie King/Pensacola News Journal

■ **RIGHT:** Volunteer James Snow (left) and Madison County Search and Rescue team members Butch Chappell (center) and Daryll Dodge discuss the areas to concentrate their search efforts, from a small command center on an on-ramp along Highway 10 in New Orleans. *Greg Pearson/The Times*

■ **FAR RIGHT:** Elizabeth Anderson and other Baptist volunteers from Florida open cans of peaches at Main Street Baptist Church in Hattiesburg, Miss.
John F. Elbers II/Rockford Register Star

■ **ABOVE:** Two-month-old Ernest James sleeps as his mother, Lewanda Stewart, searches the Web for housing. Victims of Hurricane Katrina, the New Orleans residents are staying at the Mangham Baptist Church, Mangham, La.

Ian Morrison/The News-Star

■ **ABOVE RIGHT:** Renetter Miles of New Orleans waits for a bus under the West Bank Expressway on the West Bank in New Orleans. Busses were picking up evacuees and taking them to the Astrodome in Houston, Tex.

Claudia B. Laws/The Daily Advertiser

■ **RIGHT:** Five month old Hunter Fallon sits on his mother's lap. Heather Fallon is Hunter's mom, and his great grandmother Hazel Lambert touches his hand, Monday, Sept. 12, at Woman's & Children's Hospital in Lafayette, La. Little Hunter was evacuated from Tulane Medical Center before Hurricane Katrina hit New Orleans and was brought to Womans & Childrens Hospital, but Heather did not know where he was until after the storm hit. They were reunited on Monday at the hospital.

Brad Kemp/The Daily Advertiser

■ **ABOVE:** Melissa James of Metairie, Miss. (left) and other Katrina evacuees arrive from Plaquemine to Monroe's Red Cross Shelter on Saturday, Sept. 17.
Arely D. Castillo/The News-Star

■ **ABOVE LEFT:** "I just found out my subdivision is under 4 feet of water. I think we've lost everything. I've lived in that house for 30 years. This is the first time we've ever evacuated," said Cidro Capo of St. Bernard, La., as he comforts his 3-year-old granddaughter Olivia when tornado warnings sounded off and the lights went out at the Richland High School gymnasium. Capo and five other family members heeded the call to evacuate from the path of Hurricane Katrina, joining a few hundred at the Richland shelter. *Vickie King/The Clarion-Ledger*

■ **LEFT:** Anthony Summers of Waveland, Miss., holding his granddaughter Emma Stiglets, 18 months, is at the Best Value Inn & Suites in Jackson, Miss., with six other family members. When they return to the coast, Judi will be in charge of rebuilding while her husband gets back to work with CFS Rail doing railroad maintenance, making upgrades and repairs. *Barbara Gauntt/The Clarion-Ledger*

ABOVE: Fifty-eight-year-old Johnny Mann of Gulfport, Miss., describes how Hurricane Katrina slammed into his city two weeks ago. Mann rode out the storm in his home, which is located less than half a mile from the coast. *Randy Snyder/The Herald-Dispatch*

RIGHT: Maynard Cecil Brown sits in a chair near Lee Circle in New Orleans while members of the 82nd Airborne and the Louisiana State Police talk to him about leaving the city for his own safety.
Greg Pearson/The Times

FAR RIGHT: Rollin Garcia, right, explains how he and his friend Tim Wysick helped people in their community get through Hurricane Katrina in front of Bullet's Sports and Jazz Bar near St. Augustine High School Sunday, Sept. 18.
Michael Dunlap/The News-Star

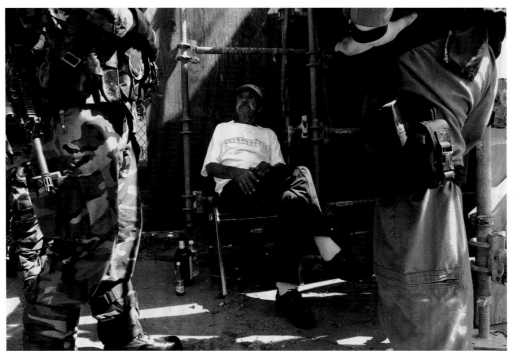

RIGHT: Margaret Fridley of New Orleans reaches out to Louisiana Gov. Kathleen Blanco as the governor tours the Red Cross Shelter at the former State Farm building in Monroe, La. Although Fridley is an evacuee, she is not a shelter resident. She came to the Red Cross for help when she saw Blanco touring the facility and asked for help. Blanco attended a prayer service and toured the shelter on Friday, Sept. 16.

Margaret Croft/The News-Star

BELOW: Mississippi Governor Haley Barbour, bottom right, answers questions during a press conference concerning the effects of Hurricane Katrina at the Emergency Operations Center of Forrest County near Hattiesburg, Miss., on Thursday, Sept. 1. In the background are Hattiesburg Mayor Johnny DuPree, left, and Billy Hudson, president of the Forrest County Board of Supervisors.

Gavin Averill/Hattiesburg American

BELOW RIGHT: Xien Huynh, a Vietnamese fisherman who lost his livelihood when Katrina destroyed his fishing boat, waits in Monroe, La., with his family.

Margaret Croft/The News-Star

■ **ABOVE:** New Orleans evacuees Shantell Antoine, her boyfriend David Harold, and their son David "Popie" Antoine, 3, share a laugh at their new apartment in Lafayette, La., on Thursday, Sept. 15. The couple were unable to get to their son on the Sunday before Hurricane Katrina hit New Orleans since the taxis had evacuated. The couple left so that Antoine could continue her dialysis and worked with the American Red Cross to find their son. The family was reunited more than two weeks later in Lafayette after "Popie" was found living with a foster family in Houston. *Claudia B. Laws/The Daily Advertiser*

■ **ABOVE LEFT:** A family is reunited at the Cajundome as two groups found each other. Derrick Bannister gives his mother Bernadette Bannister a hug after their reunion.
John Rowland/The Daily Advertiser

■ **LEFT:** Karen Oelkers Montgomery of New Orleans and her son Allyn, 9, share a smile as Montgomery's sister-in-law Yasmin Welch cooks dinner at Welch's Lafayette home. The Montgomery's have been staying with relatives in Lafayette since evacuating from their New Orleans home due to Hurricane Katrina. *Claudia B. Laws/The Daily Advertiser*

■ **ABOVE:** Hurricane Katrina evacuees Rosita Smith, left, and her great niece, Jada Rosa, 2, smile as they leave the Superdome in downtown New Orleans Saturday, Sept. 3. Evacuees were transported by bus to other shelters with better living conditions. *Jessica Leigh/The Times*

■ **FAR LEFT:** Hurricane Katrina evacuee Helen Ordon, 85, of New Orleans, is happy to be moving on from the America Red Cross shelter at the family life center at First Baptist Church of Ridgeland, Miss., in Madison County. About 20 members of her family have found apartments in Canton. "Only a couple of families and a stray cat are left here," First Baptist Pastor Grant Arinder said. Rev. Arinder said the shelter will be closed by the weekend. *Greg Jenson/The Clarion-Ledger*

■ **LEFT:** Alcorn State's head football coach Johnny Thomas (center) instructs his football players on techniques for blocking extra point and field goal attempts during practice at the University in Lorman. *Vickie King/The Clarion-Ledger*

The Recovery

It has been called "debris" and "clutter" and "rubble" — things Katrina left splintered, twisted and piled for miles along the Mississippi Gulf Coast, the more than 300,000 homes flooded in Louisiana's St. Bernard Parish and New Orleans.

But to the people who lived there, it was priceless pieces of their lives. Ruined. Gone.

Family Bibles. Photos and home movies. Wedding dresses and letter jackets. Swing sets and Christmas decorations. The program from a third-grade play.

Churches, homes, schools and businesses. Much of it left to be scooped by machines, deposited into dump trucks and hauled away by folks just doing their job, helping out. All part of the grueling, seemingly never-ending, physical recovery from Katrina.

Help arrived in all forms from across the country: Military units guarded neighborhoods from looters; Massachusetts police officers drove 3,000 miles round-trip and used vacation days to work shifts for local peers; crews from Michigan and Pennsylvania were among those who restored electricity; church groups by the dozens served food and handed out pillows and blankets at shelters.

But there is mental recovery that must take place, too. Some people lost more than stuff — they lost loved ones. Not to cancer. Not in an automobile accident. But to Mother Nature.

Others survived in the strangest of ways and questioned why. Zera Ruiz, her daughter, her brother and nine neighbors in a D'Iberville, Miss., housing project grabbed hold of a child's inflatable swimming pool and rode the surging water of Biloxi Back Bay inland to safety.

"We just floated away," a shaken Ruiz, 57, told Clarion-Ledger reporter Chris Joyner.

Rescue and recovery, we have learned, are distinctly different things.

■ **LEFT:** Grant Graham (left) with the Mississippi Crime Lab in Biloxi, Miss., leads a group of searchers looking for victims of Hurricane Katrina in the rubble of homes off U.S. 90 in Long Beach, Miss. Hurricane Katrina battered the area, destroying buildings with high wind and a large storm surge.
Rick Guy/The Clarion-Ledger

■ **RIGHT:** Manuel Vasquez, left, hugs Walt Elfert, manager of Sherwin-Williams on Magazine Street in New Orleans after the two business neighbors saw each other for the first time since Hurricane Katrina. The Sherwin-Williams store was open for business, but Elfert said that he had not had any customers all day. Business owners were allowed back into some areas of New Orleans for the first time since the hurricane. *Robert Ruiz/The Times*

■ **ABOVE:** Denise Stipe waits in line to enter the only open store in Boutte, La., a Winn-Dixie. *Claudia B. Laws/The Daily Advertiser*

■ **RIGHT:** A line forms in the parking lot of the Regions Bank on South 40th Avenue in Hattiesburg, Miss., to get free ice and water from bank employees Tuesday, Aug. 30. *Bart Boatwright/Greenville News*

■ **BELOW:** Ron Young, (left) buys supplies from Lowe's Warehouse employee Katrina Evans on Tuesday, Aug. 30. Needy residents lined up down the length of the store off Highway 98 to wait to be escorted one at a time through the store. *Joel Bonner/Hattiesburg American*

■ **LEFT:** Some waited in line more than 4 1/2 hours for their turn to shop one at a time at Walgreens in Hattiesburg, Miss. *George Clark/Hattiesburg American*

■ **BELOW:** At the Home Depot off I-55 north in Jackson, Miss., customers wait patiently for the opportunity to purchase generators and other materials to assist with wide spread power outages. Home Depot was expecting a shipment of generators from out of state. *Greg Jenson/The Clarion-Ledger*

■ **ABOVE:** New Orleans Police patrol the streets downtown looking for looters or people needing rescue. *John Rowland/The Daily Advertiser*

■ **RIGHT:** Jewel France has groceries from the looted Walgreens in the background. Police allowed people to keep items from looted stores if their bags contained only food.
John Rowland/The Daily Advertiser

■ **FAR RIGHT:** New Orleans police officer M. Wilson clears Canal Street of looters with the aid of a shot gun as Martial Law is enforced. The looter is holding a knife.
John Rowland/The Daily Advertiser

■ **ABOVE:** A New Orleans Police officer searches a man's bag for looted items on Canal Street. If police found only food in a person's bag they were allowed to keep it.
John Rowland/The Daily Advertiser

■ **RIGHT:** A team of New Orleans police officers say a prayer after clearing Canal Street of looters on Tuesday afternoon, Aug. 30. *John Rowland/The Daily Advertiser*

■ **BELOW:** Sergeant Gene Allison exits the Walgreens on Canal Street after clearing the store of looters. *John Rowland/The Daily Advertiser*

■ **LEFT:** Workers organize ways to help evacuees of Hurricane Katrina in the "war room" at the Louisiana Military Dept. Office of Homeland Security and Emergency Preparedness in Baton Rouge, La. *Jessica Leigh/The Times*

■ **BELOW:** A line of evacuees wait for lunch outside of the LSUS shelter in Shreveport, La. The sidewalk chalk writing/art on the outside walls of the building is from the evacuees staying at the facility. *Jim Hudelson/The Times*

■ RIGHT: Bus drivers pick up supplies and get their buses ready to leave. They will drive to New Orleans to get evacuees to bring them to several shelters west of the hurricane area. They left from the Northgate Mall parking lot in Lafayette, La. *Denice Broussard/The Daily Advertiser*

■ FAR RIGHT: Evacuees line up to catch a bus out of town, Thursday, Sept. 1, at the staging point on I-10 in New Orleans. *Brad Kemp/The Daily Advertiser*

■ BELOW: An elderly woman is wheeled to a waiting ambulance outside the United Pentecostal Church International Regional Office and Camp on Mississippi 18 where she and over 100 other residents and staff from the Meadow Crest Living Center in Gretna, La., had been housed since fleeing from Hurricane Katrina. Without power since Monday, searing heat took its toll on the group, claiming the life of one person and leaving several others in poor condition. The most severe cases were transported by ambulance to area hospitals while the remainder were relocated to the Mississippi Trademart in Jackson. *Joe Ellis/The Clarion-Ledger*

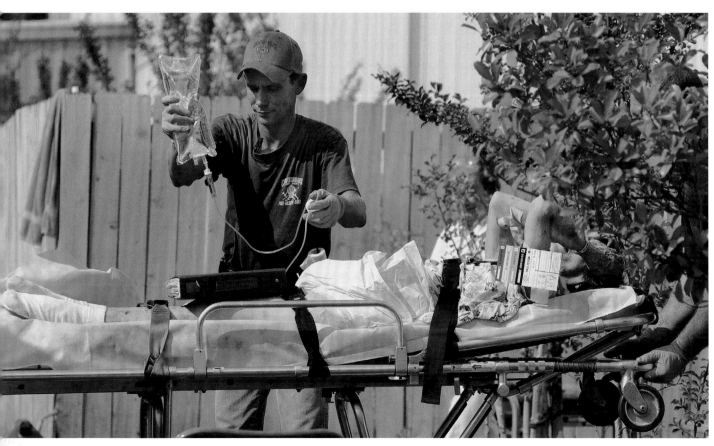

■ **ABOVE:** U.S. Coast Guard rescue searches the flooded streets of New Orleans. *Peter C. Piazza/The Daily Advertiser*

■ **RIGHT:** National Guard rescue working the flooded streets of New Orleans *Peter C. Piazza/The Daily Advertiser*

■ **FAR RIGHT:** National Guard rescue moves close to power poles and trees to make a rescue. *Peter C. Piazza/The Daily Advertiser*

■ **BELOW:** National Guard MPs move into the Superdome to help out. *Peter C. Piazza/The Daily Advertiser*

ABOVE: The massive effort to restore electrical power to areas of the state continues as Asplundh crews from as far away as Detroit, Mich., and Pennsylvania, work on a pole at School Street in Ridgeland, a suburb of Jackson, Miss.
Chris Todd/The Clarion-Ledger

LEFT: Forrest General Hospital employees in Hattiesburg, Miss., work from the command center to find places to transfer their patients in critical conditions. *Katie King/Pensacola News Journal*

FAR LEFT: Evacuees walk to the staging area in New Orleans after being brought there by a Navy helicopter, Thursday, Sept. 1. *Brad Kemp/The Daily Advertiser*

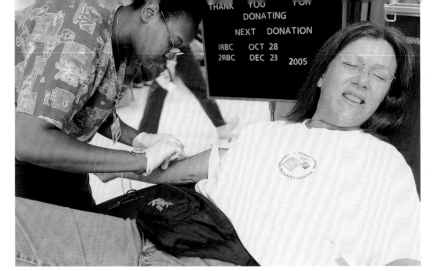

■ **ABOVE:** "I have so much scar tissue from previous donations that the first stick stings a little," said Gina Luna, a St. Dominic Hospital x-ray technician (right) as Mississippi Blood Services phlebotomist Chandra Buchanan pricks Luna's arm to begin her "gift of life" blood donation. *Vickie King/The Clarion-Ledger*

■ **LEFT:** The University of Mississippi School of Pediatric Medicine joined several other health schools in a clinic for hurricane evacuees at the Mississippi Trade Mart. Concerned parents had their children checked for illness by doctors including Dr. Jeff Crout who attempts to encourage a small child to open wide during his exam. Other specialties including dentistry, psychiatry, and infectious diseases were on hand from the University to check the patients. *J.D. Schwalm/The Clarion-Ledger*

■ **BELOW:** Vance Harris, left, of Como, Tex., and MaryAnn Parrish, community development director of the Hattiesburg Corps of the Salvation Army, pour water for David Swett, of Bowling Green, Ky., at the Salvation Army Thrift Store on Hwy. 49 in Hattiesburg, Miss., on Friday, Sept. 2. Swett, a roofer for North American Roofing, was headed toward the coast to repair roofs damaged by Hurricane Katrina. *Bill Clark/Gannett News Service*

■ **ABOVE:** Workers from L & A Contracting out of Hattiesburg, Miss., work to clear the streets of trees and debris around downtown.
Katie King/Pensacola News Journal

■ **ABOVE LEFT:** Tanker trucks wait to enter one of the gas terminals in Collins, Miss. Collins is a distribution hub for two major gasoline pipelines.
Matthew Bush/Hattiesburg American

■ **LEFT:** Capital Security guard Bobby Weathersby makes his rounds protecting the China Wok restaurant on McDowell Road in South Jackson, Miss., Friday. The entire east wall of the business collapsed in the gale force winds of Hurricane Katrina. *Vickie King/The Clarion-Ledger*

■ **ABOVE:** Buena Silve, 52, left, of Lacombe, La., complains about the lack of help from FEMA, American Red Cross and the government while waiting in line for food from kind strangers on Friday, Sept. 2. Silve said the only help the town has received arrived today from three Port St. Lucie, Fla. residents that spent $8,000 of their own money to bring people food and water.
Jessica Leigh/The Times

■ **ABOVE RIGHT:** Edward Palmer, 45, left, of Lacombe, La., gets to the front of a line to receive food from kind strangers on Friday, Sept. 2. *Jessica Leigh/The Times*

■ **RIGHT:** Standing along U.S. 51 (from left) Teresa Ware of Ridgeland, Miss., Cindy Woodall of Madison, Miss., John Murphey and wife Mollie Murphey of Madison encourage motorists to stop at a garage sale fund raiser at the Madison County Gymnastics Center, 577-a Hwy. 51, in Ridgeland. The proceeds are intended for Brook-lin Gymnastics in Pass Christian in Mississippi. The facility on the Mississippi Gulf Coast, and the home of the owner, were destroyed by Hurricane Katrina. Saturday Brook-Lin was to host their first meet.
Chris Todd/The Clarion-Ledger

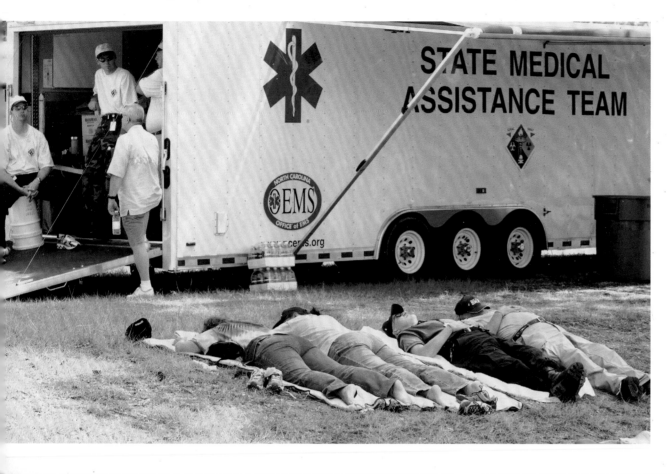

■ **LEFT:** Members of the North Carolina State Medical Assistance Team relax at Camp Shelby, outside Hattiesburg, Miss. The team paused at the base while an advance group scouted the location in Biloxi, Miss., where they will set up a 110-bed mobile hospital. *Craig Bailey/Florida Today*

■ **BELOW LEFT:** Evacuees from New Orleans receive food and water after arriving by train Saturday, Sept. 3, to Lafayette, La., before being transported to the Dallas area. *Brad Kemp/The Daily Advertiser*

■ **BELOW:** Daniel Perry waits at the boarding area for buses on I-10 at the Causeway Boulevard exit in New Orleans on Sept. 3. *John Rowland/The Daily Advertiser*

■ **RIGHT:** President George W. Bush talks with a crew from Alabama Power Co. Monday, Sept. 5, in Poplarville, Miss., as they repair electrical lines destroyed by Hurricane Katrina one week earlier.

George Clark/Hattiesburg American

■ **BELOW:** The massive effort to restore electrical power to areas of the state continues as work crews load utility poles, transformers and other equipment from this staging area on the Mississippi State Fairgrounds in Jackson.

Chris Todd/The Clarion-Ledger

■ **ABOVE:** Evacuee Dana Smith of Covington, La., is reflected in a mirrored window as she fills out an application for temporary food stamps while waiting in line at the Brandywine Executive Center in Lafayette, La. *Claudia B. Laws/The Daily Advertiser*

■ **LEFT:** Jerrold Stokes of Gulfport, Miss., finds time to wash and brush his teeth after making a trip to Florence, Miss., for relief supplies. The artesian well on Canal Road in Gulfport allowed him to safely wash. The supplies are from the Marvin United Methodist Church in Florence. *J.D. Schwalm/The Clarion-Ledger*

■ **BELOW:** Spc. Brandon Taylor (right) hands a box of baby supplies through a window of a helicopter to Staff Sgt. Charles Miller at Baton Rouge Metro Airport. The army helicopter was flown to Bogalusa, La., where diapers, infant formula and bottles were delivered. *Greg Pearson/The Times*

LEFT: Belhaven College student Kate Morgan (center), of Laurel, Miss., volunteers to pass out water to residents from various regions seeking federal assistance for Hurricane Katrina at the Red Cross shelter at the Mississippi Trade Mart in Jackson. Red Cross volunteers started handing out water after several people suffered heat exhaustion in long lines, wrapped around the Trademart. *Greg Jenson/The Clarion-Ledger*

FAR LEFT: A group of children and parents from Slidell, La., fill out registration forms at Rosa Scott Middle School in Madison, Miss., where Madison School District officials have set up a centralized registration center for students displaced by Hurricane Katrina. The group is among 23 members of El Calvario Mission Hispana church in Slidell who evacuated ahead of Hurricane Katrina and are now living at a shelter at First Baptist Church of Ridgeland, Miss. *Joe Ellis/The Clarion-Ledger*

BELOW: After more than a week off due to Hurricane Katrina, students at Ann E. Smith Elementary School returned to their Ridgeland, Miss., school on Thursday, Sept. 8. *Chris Todd/The Clarion-Ledger*

■ **ABOVE:** An armored personnel carrier with state police patrols the streets of New Orleans on Tuesday, Sept. 6. Most residents have been evacuated leaving an empty town, taken over by the military and local police. *Jessica Leigh/The Times*

■ **RIGHT:** Rescue teams continue to search for survivors and bodies by boat and helicopter in New Orleans. *Greg Pearson/The Times*

■ **ABOVE:** A sign proclaims an area of beach in Biloxi, Miss., as the U.S. Navy and U. S. Marine Corps.'s "Camp Restore." The military arrived to restore the area in the wake of Hurricane Katrina.
Karen S. Doerr/Montgomery Advertiser

■ **ABOVE LEFT:** A search and rescue team makes its way through a flooded street in New Orleans.
Greg Pearson/The Times

■ **LEFT:** Irene Gallentine searches through the rubble of her apartment for an urn holding the ashes of her neighbor's deceased husband in Long Beach, Miss. *Gavin Averill/Hattiesburg American*

■ **FAR LEFT:** Three-year-old Jacobe Moody rests in the arms of his uncle Brandon as they wait in line for food from the Salvation Army in McLain, Miss., on Sept. 6. Locals say this was the first time they had received any outside help since the hurricane.
Craig Bailey/Florida Today

■ **ABOVE:** Lewis Tree employee Jerry Kinsey, of Duplin, N.C., is served a roll by Daniel Jackson at the dining tent for utility crews at Cloverleaf Mall in Hattiesburg, Miss. The area serves as a staging and eating area for the crews, while sleeping arrangements are provided at nearby Camp Shelby.
Joel Bonner/Hattiesburg American

■ **BELOW:** Army Pfc. Brook Lindsey, right, of Fort Wayne, Ind., maintains security as 4-year-old Madyson Moody and her mother Tabatha wait to meet with the American Red Cross on Saturday, Sept. 10, at the W.U. Bill Sigler Center in Hattiesburg, Miss. Clients approved for financial assistance received a check for at least $360. Amounts varied based on the number of people living in each household prior to Hurricane Katrina. Several hundred people were turned away after appointments through Friday were booked.
Randy Snyder/The Herald-Dispatch

■ **ABOVE:** An oil worker cleans up an oil spill in flooded areas hit by Hurricane Katrina in Chalmette, La. *Claudia B. Laws/The Daily Advertiser*

■ **ABOVE RIGHT:** P.S. Energy employee Jason Waddell, of Jonesville, S.C., gasses up rows of utility trucks at the staging area for utility crews at Cloverleaf Mall in Hattiesburg, Miss. The location is used as a service and staging area and the crews are bused to Camp Shelby to spend the night. *Joel Bonner/Hattiesburg American*

■ **RIGHT:** Temble Baptist Church member Phillip Tallman offers free water to motorists passing by the corner of Hardy Street and 16th Avenue in Hattiesburg, Miss. *Natasha Smith/Hattiesburg American*

■ **ABOVE:** City of Hattiesburg employees remove a stump from Oak Lawn Cemetery, which sustained heavy tree damage during Hurricane Katrina. *John F. Elbers II/Rockford Register Star*

■ **ABOVE:** Steve Martin of H and H Storm Services of Florence, S.C., tosses a limb onto a stack of other tree debris on Monday, Sept. 12, in Hattiesburg, Miss.
Randy Snyder/The Herald-Dispatch

■ **LEFT:** Work starts on the repair of the I-10 twin spans over Lake Pontchartrain.
Peter C. Piazza/The Daily Advertiser

■ **BELOW:** Michelle Shelton (right) from USDA Rural Development's Brandon office helps Sharon Means(left), her husband Lashundo Means and their children Kiora Means (second from left), 5, and Reginald Means, 7, all of Jefferson Parish, La., fill out paper work that will allow the displaced family to move from the shelter at the Mississippi Coliseum into a home provided by the agency. *Joe Ellis/The Clarion-Ledger*

■ **ABOVE:** A front end loader pushes thousands of gallons of sludge down the street in Chalmette, La. to try and clear the streets. St. Bernard Parish officials hope that parts of the parish will open in 10 days to start rebuilding the parish infrastructure. *Shane Bevel/The Times*

FAR LEFT: An attempt at carpooling to the Salvation Army in Hattiesburg, Miss., on Tuesday, Sept. 13, proves to be a challenge as Mary Banion, left, Arlena Price, center, and Lena Carte try to load food, toiletries and cleaning supplies into Carte's convertible. The trio, who each filed separate claims for suffering losses from Hurricane Katrina, traveled back to Collins in the over-stuffed car. *Randy Snyder/ The Herald-Dispatch*

ABOVE LEFT: A long line of storm victims wait at a Red Cross assistance center at the Mississippi Trademart in Jackson. *Joe Ellis/The Clarion-Ledger*

LEFT: Electricity is gradually being restored to parts of the Gulf Coast by workers like these, fixing power lines a few blocks off U.S. 90 on the beach in Gulfport, Miss. *Rick Guy/The Clarion-Ledger*

■ **ABOVE:** Bergen County Sheriff's Corrections Officer Chris Olivo stands guard at the rear of a group from the New Jersey Task Force 1 search and rescue team as they conduct a house-to-house search in a previously flooded neighborhood on Hamilton Street in New Orleans on Tuesday, Sept. 13. *Gavin Averill/Hattiesburg American*

■ **LEFT:** U.S. Navy ships dock in New Orleans with relief supplies and help. *Peter C. Piazza/The Daily Advertiser*

■ **ABOVE:** Tasha (right), 25, and Garret Lamson, 26, of Lafayette, La., sing during a candlelight vigil hosted by United Campus Ministries for those who have been affected by Hurricane Katrina at the University of Louisiana in Lafayette.
Claudia B. Laws/The Daily Advertiser

■ **FAR LEFT:** National Guardsmen patrol the empty streets of the French Quarter in New Orleans. *Peter C. Piazza/The Daily Advertiser*

■ **LEFT:** Dakayla Harris, 5, carries a box of food donated to her family by Feed the Children and Operation Rebound at Mt. Carmel Baptist Church in Hattiesburg, Miss., on Thursday, Sept 15. Representatives from Feed the Children and professional basketball players were on hand to meet local residents and distribute food and supplies to citizens affected by Hurricane Katrina. *Gavin Averill/Hattiesburg American*

FAR LEFT: Heading down I-55 in Jackson, Miss., the Operation Rebound caravan of 18-wheelers carries emergency supplies for residents affected by Katrina in Hattiesburg, Miss., and on the Mississippi Gulf Coast. The partnership between the National Basketball Players Association and the international relief organization Feed the Children features former and current NBA and WNBA players, including, Al Jefferson, Swin Cash, Justin Reed, Clarence Weatherspoon, Eric Dampier, Mo Williams, Purvis Short, Greg Anthony, Theo Ratliff and others. Twenty-three trucks carried emergency relief for over 5,000 people.
Greg Jenson/The Clarion-Ledger

LEFT: Hazmat workers from Bengal Enterprises clear out the food from a restaurant near Bourbon Street in the French Quarter of New Orleans.
Shane Bevel/The Times

■ **ABOVE:** Louisiana National Guardsmen from Monroe, La., patrol the dust filled streets of Arabi, La., after the deep mud has dried. *Peter C. Piazza/The Daily Advertiser*

■ **LEFT:** Louisiana National Guardsmen from Monroe, La., push mud and sludge out of the streets of Arabi, La., after the area was flooded by a levee break. *Peter C. Piazza/The Daily Advertiser*

■ **BELOW:** Rev. Terry R. Pannell talks to Maria Vallejo, of Honduras, at the end of service at St. Alban's Episcopal Church on Sunday, Sept. 18, in Monroe, La. Vallejo and her family lived in Kenner, La., and are Katrina evacuees. *Arely D. Castillo/The News-Star*

■ **ABOVE:** Betty Jean James of Monroe, La., organizes clothes for Katrina evacuees at Rays of Sonshine on Saturday, Sept. 17, in Monroe. *Arely D. Castillo/The News-Star*

■ **RIGHT:** Harri Haikala breaks out molded sheetrock in his brother-in-law's home in the University area of New Orleans Sunday, Sept. 18. *Michael Dunlap/The News-Star*

■ **FAR RIGHT:** Gail Marie, singer and owner of Guidry Cleaning Service, has put her music career on hold to help restaurants get back to business in New Orleans. Marie is pictured here Monday, Sept. 19. *Michael Dunlap/The News-Star*

■ **ABOVE:** Jayshon Davis (left), 1, of Jackson, Miss., gets acquainted with Jackson Police officer Lance Scott while the line to pick up tickets for appointments for Hurricane Katrina disaster assistance at the Mississippi Trademart curves pass the Mississippi Coliseum. Scott said participants were in good spirits because the lines moved faster.   *Greg Jenson/The Clarion-Ledger*

■ **LEFT:** Dr. Thomas Trieu of Ocean Springs, Miss., scatters soggy charts from his water logged medical practice. His offices received major damage and he doesn't know when he will be able to resume his practice.   *J.D. Schwalm/The Clarion-Ledger*

■ **ABOVE:** Workers with CK1 Contracting of Tenn., (from left) Darryl Hanner, Todd Wilcox and Darryll Julian, load debris from a damaged home into a dump truck on East Street in Pass Christian, Miss. *Rick Guy/The Clarion-Ledger*

■ **LEFT:** Drew Kern, of Hattiesburg, Miss., lures customers to Shipley Do-Nuts on Saturday, Sept. 3, as the store opens for the first time since Hurricane Katrina hit the region. The Kern family, owners of the shop, had evacuated to Tupelo, Miss., before the storm. With electric power slowly being restored to the area, the Kerns were able to re-open Saturday morning as more businesses tried to return to normal operations. *Bill Clark/Gannett News Service*

■ **FAR LEFT:** Janet Saxer cleans up debris around her home at 134 Farrar Lane in Waveland, Miss. Saxer and her husband are living in a trailer donated by FEMA on the foundation of their home that was destroyed during Hurricane Katrina. *Jim Hudelson/The Times*

■ **ABOVE:** Todd Lively, general manager of the Three-Legged Dog Tavern, was one of the first to begin serving hot meals in the French Quarter which opened for residents to return. Lively has to truck in everything from meat to potable water to keep the bar open. *Shane Bevel/The Times*

■ **RIGHT:** Sheppard Bowman stands in his doorway at 3004 Jacob Drive in Chalmette, La., where he is ankle deep in sludge and oil that was spilled from Murphy Oil Corp. after Hurricane Katrina. The brown marking on Bowman's doorway is the level the oil reached in his house and throughout his street, which sits one block from Murphy Oil Corp. *Robert Ruiz/The Times*

■ **BELOW:** Workers spray water into a canal along Jacob Drive in Chalmette, La., to move spilled oil down the canal toward skimmers. The oil was spilled from the Murphy Oil Corp. after Hurricane Katrina hit the Louisiana Coast. *Robert Ruiz/The Times*

The Future

For people who have lost everything, the future can be reduced to the next day. Will there be enough food? What does Mother Nature next have in store? Where will they be living? Will they be living?

They have learned life's uncertainties the hard way and react to any talk of next year or 10 years from now like a toddler touching a hot stove. They can't see past the current pain. Tomorrow can wait.

But, in reality, it can't.

"To build a stronger, more resilient and prosperous Gulf Coast, you have to know what to build, where to build and how to build," said Harriet Tregoning, executive director of Smart Growth America in Washington, D.C. "A couple of years of not knowing where and what to build will be very devastating."

The cold truth is, Katrina's powerful surge and floodwaters erased much of the Mississippi Gulf Coast and parts of New Orleans. It is virtually a clean slate for builders, planners and dreamers.

The Mississippi Renewal Forum, part of Gov. Haley Barbour's Commission on Recovery, Rebuilding and Renewal, has presented cities and residents staggering plans for a "new" Coast. It would resemble Seaside, Fla., one of the leaders in New Urbanism, a return to the traditional neighborhood with consistent architecture — even the local Wal-Marts — and strict building codes, featuring both cosmetic and safety demands.

Plans include a rail system connecting coastal cities, lots of green spaces, scenic routes along the beaches to reduce traffic.

Each city is free to choose its own destiny. Building would be financed primarily through private investors.

Such plans were presented after Hurricane Camille ravaged the Coast in 1969. None was implemented. Barbour doesn't want Mississippi to repeat its mistake. "In no time they were building gas stations on the beach," he said. "I want to make sure we get it right this time."

In New Orleans, Mayor C. Ray Nagin is facing one of the most unique problems in modern history: How do you rebuild a city that ranked in the top 35 in population?

Initial plans imposed a four-month building moratorium and created a new authority that could use eminent domain to seize private property in flooded areas that won't be rebuilt.

Affected residents reacted angrily. Some said they would rather die on their tiny plot of land than have it taken from them. It's home, they screamed.

Others see it as a city that once was. New Orleans had a population of 462,000 before Katrina's floodwaters forced about 300,000 to evacuate. Many have chosen to make a new life elsewhere. The Rand Corporation estimates the city, if it's lucky, could grow to 247,000 by 2008 — still a fraction of its old self.

What the Mississippi Gulf Coast and New Orleans will look like in 20 years is anybody's guess.

But regardless of whether officials and residents want to accept it, the future is in their tired hands.

■ **LEFT:** New Orleans Mayor Ray Nagin pauses during a press conference at the Sheraton on Canal Street. The mayor introduced a commission of 17 community leaders to aid him in rebuilding New Orleans.
Shane Bevel/The Times

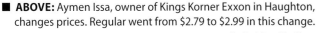

■ **ABOVE:** Aymen Issa, owner of Kings Korner Exxon in Haughton, changes prices. Regular went from $2.79 to $2.99 in this change. *Jim Hudelson/The Times*

■ **RIGHT:** Gasoline prices at the Chevron station along U.S. Hwy 80 in Bossier City, La., near the intersection of I-220. *Jim Hudelson/The Times*

■ **FAR RIGHT:** The Pontchartrain Causeway carries traffic into and out of Jefferson Parish and the city of New Orleans. The city has suspended its reopening in anticipation of a possible hit from Tropical Storm Rita, currently nearing the Florida Keys. *Shane Bevel/The Times*

RIGHT: Pat Dugan makes his rounds through the New Orleans Museum of Art in City Park with Louisiana State Police SWAT team member Scott Spencer. Dugan and nearly a dozen other NYPD officers were contracted by Lloyd's of London to secure and protect the priceless art in the museum after Hurricane Katrina. *Shane Bevel/The Times*

BELOW: Workers put the final touches on the FEMA trailer city in Baker, La., in preparation for evacuees from New Orleans and the surrounding areas. The camp has nearly 600 trailers that each will house up to four people. *Shane Bevel/The Times*

BELOW RIGHT: New Orleans locals Larry Loga Jr. and his girlfriend Susie Hess dance at The Famous Door on Bourbon Street. The club was one of many that reopened this weekend in the French Quarter. *Shane Bevel/The Times*

■ **ABOVE:** A National Guard soldier passes by the Desire Oyster Bar on Bourbon Street. The restaurant is one of a handful on the famous street that reopened this weekend and began serving food and drink. *Shane Bevel/The Times*

■ **LEFT:** Fortune teller Bruce Wilson talks to clients on Bourbon Street on Saturday night. Wilson is one of the first street performers to return to the French Quarter in New Orleans. *Shane Bevel/The Times*

■ **ABOVE:** Bourbon Street and the rest of the French quarter opened again to residents and emergency workers. *Shane Bevel/The Times*

ABOVE: Brenda Kitchens of Pascagoula, Miss., sifts through sand at her sister-in-law's home, 823 Beach Boulevard in Pascagoula, looking for items to recover.
Rick Guy/The Clarion Ledger

ABOVE LEFT: As Kelly Moses (center) washes out baby bottles in what is left of her home, Josh Pino (left) and Don Marcheschi (right), building inspectors for the city of Sacramento, Calif., inspect the Ocean Springs, Miss., house. Kelly had just given birth two weeks before Hurricane Katrina when she had to evacuate with her husband and their son, Brian. *Barbara Gauntt/The Clarion Ledger*

LEFT: After removing the fuel, U.S. Coast Guard subcontractors Charleston Marine of Charleston, S.C., and Beyel Brothers Crane Inc. of Cocoa, Fla., work on extricating the shrimp boat Sea Lover grounded during Hurricane Katrina in Industrial Canal, just east of Loraine Cowan Road in Gulfport, Miss. A harbor oil boom sits in the water to catch any remaining fuel and to help protect workers from incoming wakes from passing vessels. According to U.S. Coast Guard MST1 Matt Valenti of Seattle, Wa., their crew will be removing about 25 vessels within a three mile stretch. A larger crane is expected within a few days to handle bigger boats. *Barbara Gauntt/The Clarion Ledger*

■ **ABOVE:** With Hurricane Rita bearing down on the Gulf Coast, work continues on repairing the 17th Street Canal levee in New Orleans. The U.S. Army Corps of Engineers has a plan in place to seal the canal from the lake with a sheet pile wall to protect the weakened levee from any possible rising water due to Hurricane Rita. *Shane Bevel/The Times*

■ **RIGHT:** Gov. Kathleen Blanco speaks with New Orleans Mayor Ray Nagin during a press conference at the Sheraton on Canal Street where the mayor introduced a commission of 17 community leaders to aid him in rebuilding New Orleans. *Shane Bevel/The Times*

■ **FAR RIGHT:** A bulldozer spreads gravel along the top of the 17th Street Canal in New Orleans. Repairs are being made to the levee and plans to block water flowing from the lake with a sheet pile wall are already in the works to prevent a second storm surge from destroying the patch. *Shane Bevel/The Times*

RIGHT: Teacher Elka Michalak works to illustrate probabilities to students during a math session. The Lowden Foundation has set up a temporary tent school with volunteer teachers at the Bay High Sports Complex. Math, story time, computers and art are part of the educational enrichment activities for the children. *J.D. Schwalm/The Clarion Ledger*

BELOW RIGHT: With phone service still out in areas due to Hurricane Katrina, Anita Adcox (center) of Picayune, Miss., Kumi Grenham (left) of Nicholson, Miss., and Joe Fortenberry (right) of Picayune use BellSouth phones in downtown Picayune. *Barbara Gauntt/The Clarion Ledger*

BELOW: Mark Smith of Long Beach, Miss., makes his way through the debris of the First Baptist Church in Long Beach Saturday. He joined his son, Brandon, 18, a student at Mississippi State University who was visiting the church for the first time since the storm. Smith was married in the church and his son was baptized in the structure. The destructive force of Hurricane Katrina swept through the churches along the Mississippi Gulf Coast ripping through walls and flooding houses of worship. Churches and their congregations have adjusted to the loss of their buildings and worked to restore a sense of normalcy with the holding of services in alternative locations. *J.D. Schwalm/The Clarion Ledger*

■ ABOVE: Plenty of repair help appears to be available for property and homeowners according to the signs posted at many intersections all along the devastated region of the Mississippi Gulf Coast. This large group of signs was found in the Gulf Hills area of Ocean Springs, Miss. *Vickie D. King/The Clarion Ledger*

■ LEFT: Mandi Bloom-Haas of Bay St. Louis, Miss., takes her pekin duck "Mack" for a stroll Monday afternoon. While her home flooded in 6 feet of water, she said she, her husband and her pets were all safe in Florida when Hurricane Katrina hit Bay St. Louis. *Brian Albert Broom/The Clarion Ledger*

■ BELOW: Louisiana evacuee Karen Pelas (left), her husband Mark and their daughter Gracie (right), 4, have been living in a borrowed camper at Percy Quin State Park in McComb, Miss., since early September. The owners of the camper need it back, so the Pelas family will be living in a tent on the site. According to Pelas, they and other Hurricane Katrina evacuees living at the park, who either bought or were loaned campers, are required to pay rent on the camp site. Evacuees living in FEMA trailers don't pay rental fees. *Barbara Gauntt/The Clarion Ledger*

■ **ABOVE:** Danny Luck (left) and Cliff Comeaux work to save a shrimp catch on a boat in Delcambre, La., by deheading them and freezing them. After Hurricanes Katrina and Rita there are no wholesalers left in Delcambreto buy them. The shrimp will be sold for nearly a third their normal price. *Shane Bevel/The Times*

■ **FAR LEFT:** Captain Ray Billiot, from Bay St. Louis, Miss., (left) works with Nac Sebin and other shrimpers to save a catch of 30 boxes. *Shane Bevel/The Times*

■ **LEFT:** Shrimper Dennis Martin rides down the canal in Delcambre after checking on his shrimp boat. Martin, from Lafourche Parish, La., rode the storm out in Lafayette, La., and came back to make sure his boat was OK. Since the season was ruined by the storms, he says he will return to Lafourche Parish for the rest of the season. *Shane Bevel/The Times*

■ **ABOVE:** Sercompce Haynes of Aerotek removes debris from North Bay Elementary in Bay St. Louis, Miss., where children returned to classes in portable buildings after Hurricane Katrina destroyed their school. *Brian Albert Broom/The Clarion Ledger*

■ **RIGHT:** What is deemed as household debris is amassed in a nearly 30-ft. high mound by Army Corps of Engineer workers at the Henley Site in Kiln, Miss. *Vickie D. King/The Clarion Ledger*

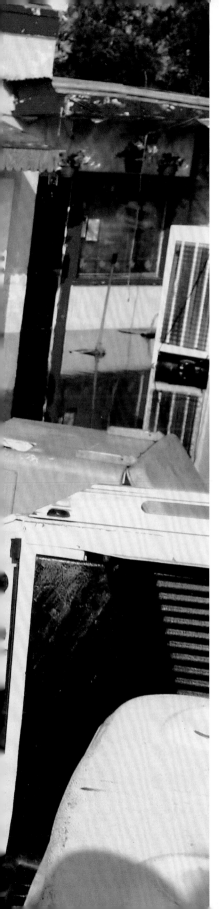

■ **ABOVE & FAR LEFT:** Lance Romero rinses off his hands in the floodwaters of Hurricane Rita after helping his father Phillip clean out the freezers at Bridgeside Seafood. Phillip, who bought the company shortly after Hurricane Lili, says that he will reopen when he can find a place to buy seafood and get his freezers working. *Shane Bevel/The Times*

■ **LEFT:** Louisiana Gov. Kathleen Blanco speaks about her state's need for federal assistance with local parish payrolls during a press conference in the Louisiana State Capitol. With little or no tax base left in the aftermath of Hurricanes Katrina and Rita, many parishes will be forced to lay off employees. *Shane Bevel/The Times*

■ **ABOVE:** The barge of the Palace Casino in Biloxi, Miss., sits at an angle after being damaged by the storm surge and high wind from Hurricane Katrina. *Rick Guy/The Clarion Ledger*

■ **LEFT:** Jonathan Cecil of Pascgoula, Miss., fishes on the jetty at Pascagoula as the Carnival Holiday cruise ship pulls into port. The ship, which has housed approximately 1300 Hurricane Katrina evacuees since September, left its berth in Mobile, Ala., to relocate to Pascagoula where many of the evacuees are working. Cecil said he has been staying on the ship, but decided to fish while waiting for it to arrive rather than take the trip. *Rick Guy/The Clarion Ledger*

■ **LEFT:** Long Beach students Dart Spiers (left) and Elizabeth Maloy work on a homecoming float as they prepare for joint homecoming festivities with Pass Christian High Shool. *Rick Guy/The Clarion Ledger*

RIGHT: "Can't be waiting on FEMA, but I got to. My house has come a long way, no thanks to FEMA. I got this right here taken care of myself," said Betty Harry of Gulfport, Miss., in a partially repaired portion of her kitchen. "I got ahold of FEMA at the end of August. I'm still waiting on that trailer. Now, today, there he is across the street, next door and here I am and he tells me he'll try to fit me in.""This man", said Harry, pointing to a FEMA representative parked at a neighbor's house across the street, "is gonna tell me he'll try and work me in. After all this and here I am waiting. He tells me he couldn't reach me with the phone number he has for me-when they know nobody stays here. Look at it, it's unliveable. Look, I called FEMA and gave them my change in phone numbers. So my address matches up, but not the phone numbers. Now look, there he goes, ain't this something," said Betty Harry of the Villa Del Ray subdivision in Gulfport, as she watches a FEMA representative stop in on her neighbor's and not her Friday. *Vickie D. King/The Clarion Ledger*

FAR RIGHT: Kathy Brugger-Volkman looks over the remains of her parents's home, Harbour Oaks, on W. Scenic Drive in Pass Christian, Miss., while her husband, John Volkman, holds up a lamp he's found. Her father was killed when the house collapsed during the storm and her mother survived by holding on to a tree. *Rick Guy/The Clarion Ledger*

■ **ABOVE:** With her new home in the background, Mercille Wilkinson of Waveland, Miss., gets food for the few local raccoons that survived Hurricane Katrina. While the 32 foot RV is a bit cramped for her and her husband, Walter Wilkinson, both are happy to be out of a shelter. *Brian Albert Broom/The Clarion Ledger*

■ **LEFT:** Gary Reid of Austin, Tex., says he plans on making Mississippi his new home after he saw the need for assistance on the Gulf Coast. He arrived a few days after Katrina hit, working to help in anyway he can. He has been amazed at the volunteers traveling from across the country to help. "At last count we had 44 states and several foreign countries pass through the area." Some of the volunteers added their hometowns to a small sign at the Fox's Den distribution site in Pass Christian, Miss.
J.D. Schwalm/The Clarion Ledger

■ **FAR LEFT:** Cathy Dumal, interim clinic director at Camp Coast Care in Long Beach, Miss., says there is a need for additional medicines including over-the-counter medicines like Zicam. However, those needs change daily. The medicine needs of Camp Coast Care vary from day to day. One day they can have an abundance of medicine for an injury and the next needing more. The site treats an average of 160 people a day, the majority needing treatment for puncture wounds or respiratory infections. *J.D. Schwalm/The Clarion Ledger*

■ **ABOVE:** Bradley Randall, the Biology Project Coordinator/Shellfish for the Mississippi Department of Marine Resources, is heartened by the apparent good "spat set" just prior to the storm. Juvenile oysters are growing on material in the sound including old tires. However, Hurricane Katrina caused an estimated 95 percent mortality rate for marketable oysters in the Mississippi Sound. It takes 18 months to three years for the small oysters to grow to market size (about three inches).
J.D. Schwalm/The Clarion Ledger

■ **RIGHT:** Jerry Ross of Waveland, Miss., surfaces from the debris of his home with a sign reading "God Keeps His Promises." Trying to find a few of his belongings before his lot is cleared, Ross and some friends cut holes through the debris so he could get underneath. Ross said he plans to take the sign to his heavily damaged church, First Baptist Church of Bay St. Louis, Miss. *Brian Albert Broom/The Clarion Ledger*

■ **ABOVE:** Leslie Bonfiglio of Lucedale, Miss., says she is glad Imperial Palace reopened as she joined thousands of others who came for the first day of gaming on the Coast since Hurricane Katrina made landfall more than three months earlier. *Brian Albert Broom/The Clarion Ledger*

■ **LEFT:** The Isle of Capri in Biloxi, Miss., reopened its doors to the public making it the first casino south of U.S. 90 to offer gaming since Hurricane Katrina. The 900 slots, 27 table games and nine poker tables were packed with patrons wanting to try their luck and skill. *J.D. Schwalm/The Clarion Ledger*

■ **ABOVE LEFT:** Stroke victim George Johnson, 63, has been shuffled from shelter to shelter since Hurricane Katrina. At times he stays with his brother, sleeping in the tent behind him. The house is tarp covered and leaks. *Barbara Gauntt/The Clarion Ledger*

■ ABOVE: Pete Sones of Pascagoula, Miss., says he misses his home as he strings Christmas lights on his trailer. Despite the complete destruction of his house by Hurricane Katrina, he says he will rebuild but has no idea how long the process will take.
Brian Albert Broom/The Clarion Ledger

■ ABOVE RIGHT: The stress of the past four months is hitting Joanne Eldridge, a resident of Scenic Trails RV Park in rural Hancock County. She, her husband and their 14-year-old daughter live in a FEMA trailer at the RV park that sits nowhere near regular conveniences like food stores and gas stations. Inside the trailer is the smallest tree they've ever had. Outside the trailer is a tent decorated with Christmas lights. According to Eldridge, children have to catch the school bus around 6:30 am and don't get home until after dark. Her daughter is in special education. Eldridge drives 45 minutes to take her to school in Gulfport, Miss., so her progress isn't interrupted. *Barbara Gauntt/The Clarion Ledger*

■ RIGHT: Residents line up for free presents at Compassion Central on Division Street in Biloxi, Miss. *Brian Albert Broom/The Clarion Ledger*

■ **ABOVE:** Dorothy Allen of Pass Christian, Miss., gazes out the door of her FEMA trailer amid rows of others at Pass Christian's Five Star Resort campground. SInce moving into the trailer after her house was destroyed by Hurricane Katrina, Allen has been frustrated by conditions at the campground. *Joe Ellis/The Clarion Ledger*

■ **ABOVE LEFT:** A playful sign greets people at a downtown Pass Christian tent city that houses residents left without shelter in the wake of Hurricane Katrina. *Joe Ellis/The Clarion Ledger*

■ **LEFT:** Brenda Carr, office manager for D & H Marine in Gulfport, Miss., says the boats damaged by Hurricane Katrina were all shapes and sizes. Power boats and sail boats that have been totaled by insurance companies will be auctioned off. Thousands of water craft damaged by Hurricane Katrina are now at the scrap yard or on the auction block. Nearly 300 water craft, from jet skis to yachts, are being prepared for auction. *J.D. Schwalm/The Clarion Ledger*

■ **ABOVE:** Mississippi Air National Guard Staff Sgt. Clarisse Marie Saucier of Pass Christian, Miss., directs traffic at the intersection of U.S. 90 and DuBuys Road in Biloxi, Miss. A stretch of U.S. 90 from DuBuys west to U.S. 49 in Gulfport, Miss., was recently re-opened to the public. *Joe Ellis/The Clarion Ledger*

■ **RIGHT:** U.S. Air Force Master Sgt. Ralph Fries looks at the Ocean Springs-Biloxi Bridge destroyed by Hurricane Katrina. Some fear the lack of the bridge is losing potential business for Ocean Springs, Miss.
Brian Albert Broom/The Clarion Ledger

■ **BELOW:** Hurricane Katrina caused heavy damage to the road and property in Pascagoula, Miss. Barricades keeps traffic off a section of Beach Boulevard near Washington Avenue. *Greg Jenson/The Clarion Ledger*